NEW LEAF

Ugly Me: Book 3

J.E. Stamper

Rehm to Kristin

I greatly appreciate you taking the time to read my book. Please consider leaving a review wherever
you bought the book and telling your friends about it.

Thank you so much for your support.

For Mom and Dad, my original fans.

Want more?

Check out the free prequel story!

Click below to receive a free eBook and audiobook version!

https://www.jestamper.com/sign-up

CHAPTER 1

The ramshackle buildings lining the street disappear in a blur as I jet past. The loose sole of my shoe catches on something and rips off like a big, dirty scab. Little rocks and bits of street crud bite into the bottom of my unprotected foot, leaving behind little pinpricks of hot pain.

But I can't let the hurt slow me down. If I slow down even for a second, well, I don't want to think about what would happen then.

No no no no! Panic sinks in and digs its sharp talons deep into my head. My ticker kicks it up another notch and tries to hammer its way out of my ribcage so hard my whole chest hurts.

I keep running like a scared bunny, *hop, hurt, hop, hurt,* until my holey sock is damp with blood. I can hear the *squish squish,* and I know without looking that I'm blazing a trail of red even a blind man could follow.

Not good. Not good at all.

No chance to hide my way out of this one.

His hot breath reeks like liquor and some other kind of mean stink. It's puffing out of him in ragged gasps as he closes the gap between us. If it wasn't for this stupid foot, I could hope to run him into a heart attack or at least out-tough him.

But not now.

I like to play the role of the tough girl, a street-hardened graduate cum laude of The School of Hard Knocks. But when it comes down to it, I'm just a hurt, scared little girl.

Each step is a fresh agony.

I'd shout for help, but my legs and heart are drinking up every bit of oxygen and screaming for more, more, more. Not that it would do any good to scream. The faces that whiz by are so wrapped up in their own crappy existences they don't even look up from their phones and cigarettes.

I don't have to look back to know he's getting closer, that the end of little old me is getting closer. They say that before you die, your life flashes before your eyes. But right now the only things flashing before my eyes are dingy, dilapidated houses and muddy front yards cluttered with garbage.

But I guess that is my life. *Was* my life, anyway.

Garbage. Dumpster Girl. Ugly Me.

I hear a siren in the distance. For a split-second, a little trickle of hope seeps in. But it dries up as the sounds disappear into the distance.

His hand brushes the hair streaming out behind me. Almost gets a grip on it, but a few strands tug painfully loose. He grunts in frustration.

This is it. This is really it.

Church people sing songs about Heaven like they can't wait to skedaddle out of this life and get there. Sounds pretty good to me right now. I went to this church a couple times before they ran me out, and this woman would shout-sing all off-key with tears streaming down her wrinkled face. This other guy told me later that the lady used to be an almost famous writer from somewhere in the West. Until one day while she was out at a book signing or something this tornado came along and, *boom*, flattened her house and killed all her family. Totally lost it after that and moved out here.

Never wrote another word. Now she shows up to church every time and sings and cries and waits.

"A perfect example of unwavering faith," the guy said, dabbing at his eyes with an old red bandana. "Even in the face of such adversity, she never stopped believing in a brighter future. An inspiration to us all. Like a modern-day Job right here in our congregation."

Totally certain. No doubt in her mind.

Not me. I'm full of doubts and fears and uncertainties and all sorts of other non-good thoughts all swirling around in my noggin all the time. Peck-peck-pecking at me like a flock of hungry crows. Or what's the name for a group of crows?

A *murder*. How appropriate.

The only thing I'm certain of is that no matter what happens, I'm totally screwed.

And if I was even half-certain that there was something better waiting for me on the big, mysterious "other side," I might not try as hard to stick around on this crappy side. Take my chances and just let go. Not like that thought hadn't crossed my mind a few times over the years. But I find it hard to believe that there's a God who supposedly loves kids like me but lets them grow up hungry and hurting and thrown away like garbage. Knowing my luck, what comes next would be worse than what I've got now.

If that's even possible.

I mean, if God can make a place like Heaven for after people die, then why can't life here be, I don't know, *not* totally horrible?

I don't have time to contemplate because the rough hand wraps itself in my hair and yanks back.

My screams get choked out as he tightens his grip around my throat.

CHAPTER 2

My screams last for a few more seconds after Carol flicks on the light and wraps her arms around me.

She shushes me with a gentle hiss like a tire leaking air. I push against her for a second, trying to break her grip on me because I'm still dream-scared and locked in that weird asleep/awake purgatory.

She just squeezes me tighter into the front of her paisley nightgown. "It's alright, dear. It's alright. You're safe and sound here with me."

The bedroom finally comes into focus as the terrordream fades into the background. I squeeze my eyes closed as tears leak out and dampen the soft, age-worn cloth of her gown.

She rocks gently as her hand moves to stroke the back of my sweaty head. "You have that nightmare again?"

I nod, rubbing my snotty nose against her like a little baby or something. I drink in her scent—white bar soap and a flowery detergent. A clean smell. I choke back a sneeze. The urge isn't as strong as it used to be. Guess I'm getting used to it.

The smell of clean, that is.

She pulls away and wipes at my cheeks with her knobby fingers. "The man with the oddly shaped head?"

I shake my head and take a big, sobbing breath.

"Your father?"

I nod. A scared little puppy whimper squeaks out of me, and I bury myself into her again. Sometimes it's him. Sometimes it's the man with the weird head. Sometimes it's my mom's ex who tried to feel me up on the sofa while she was asleep.

She starts rocking again. I breathe deep into the motion, trying to quiet my hammering heart.

"You needn't be afraid any longer, Miranda." She pulls away and cups my face between her hands. "You're with me now, and I'm going to take care of you."

I nod and close my eyes to dam another flood. A wave of nausea threatens to rush in and steal this moment away from me. I peel her hands away and lay back on the bed. Deep breath in, hold, deep breath out, hold— just like I learned last week in therapy. Trying to calm the massive earthquake in my chest.

So soft, so warm. Just outside the window, a chill October breeze tickles the bare branches of the giant oak in the yard. But no matter how hard or cold the wind blows, it can't touch me in here. Carol's house has no broken windows or cracks or rotten boards. No scurrying of insects when I flick on the lights. I don't wake up scratching at little red welts. Downstairs, a fridge full of food drones on. There's no hidden stash of dusty ramen packets under that one. On it, faded cartoon piggy magnets hold notes and reminders, their plastic smiles permanent and unwavering even after God knows how many years of service. When I first got here, Carol had to constantly fuss at me because I'd open the thing a million times a day and just stand there and look at all the stuff in it.

But it's been a month, and I'm still afraid to smile. Like I'm still not comfortable being comfortable or something. Still scared to freaking death that this whole thing is just a pleasant and fleeting dream, that the horrible nightmares I still have almost every night are my reality now and forever. Don't trust myself to settle in and be nice and happy because I'm afraid I couldn't handle it if all this got suddenly taken away from me.

If that happened, if I let myself think that this is where I belong only to get yanked away like a rotten tooth in a mouthful of pearly whites—well, I think it would destroy me once and for all.

There'd be no coming back, then. It'd be Ugly Me forever and always no matter what. I've learned to live with the constant ache of deprivation. But I couldn't survive the death blow of a new life ripped away from me. Easier to live without something in the first place than to have it and suddenly lose it.

Carol's finger traces the smooth space above my eyebrows. Her fingertip is rough, weathered by years of work in the yard and garden. Wouldn't be surprised to find out she grew up on a farm. She hums some song I don't recognize, but it sounds old-fashioned, like something soldiers in dress khakis and their sweethearts would dance to before all the men in town loaded up to fight in some faraway war.

Some distant memory stirs from the dim vaults of my Before. Mom's soft touch drawing circles on the sun-browned skin of my back. I'd taken a tumble from a tree and ended up with a fractured wrist. The hurt kept me awake, but her caresses sent the pain away and soothed me to sleep. After things got bad, I sometimes wondered if I could hurt myself bad enough to bring back that version of her. I'd have done anything, even just for a few more minutes of that.

I tried a few times, but it just made her mad at me. The pain only added more scars to my tally.

Her finger moves down the line of my jaw. A smile tiptoes into the corner of my mouth, a shy little one testing the waters.

I pinch it down.

Her finger screeches to a halt, and she lets out a quiet little wheesh of air. A disappointed noise. We remain locked in this silence for a moment. She moves to get up, but I grab her hand.

I know what she's thinking, and as scary as it is to say something, I can't let her leave like that. She deserves more than that.

"It's not you, you know." My voice crackles with teary static. "I just want you to know that. It's not you. You're amazing, and I'm so thankful for everything. It's just that—that—" I can't finish. The words get all gummed up inside me.

A relieved sigh. Her full weight rests on the bed again. "Thank you for saying that, dear." Her hand moves to stroke my hair. "I know it must be a difficult adjustment. Just give it some time."

Time. That's exactly what I'm worried about.

Because no matter how good things are right now, I can't escape the feeling that I'm living inside some kind of giant ticking clock.

And I'm scared to death of what's going to happen when the last seconds tick by.

CHAPTER 3

I don't even bother trying to sleep after all that. What with the afterimages of the nightmare imprinted on my eyes and all the other worries running circles about my brain, getting any quality shuteye is out of the question. Besides, the old clock on the nightstand says it's 3:48. Too early to get up and get ready for the day, too late to get enough extra sleep to not wake up all groggy and grumpy. The clock's one of those deals with the little plastic card things that flip down when the minutes and hours change. Actually pretty darn cool. The room itself is pretty standard old lady chic with a 1970's flair. Lots of faded brownish floral prints on top of a puke green and burnt orange color scheme. Even though this stuff is probably a lot older than my mom, it's cleaner and in better shape than pretty much anything I can ever remember having. The room has this whole look of a place made up perfect for someone that never came to live in it.

The only thing out of place is this old sticker on the plastic fake woodgrain of the clock's side. It's super faded and is mostly ripped off, but I can just make out the half-smile of a red-haired cartoon girl with a pink bonnet. Very odd. Makes me wonder if Carol maybe bought the clock secondhand or something. She's never mentioned anything about having kids of her own. No adult children call or come by to visit. This little shred of a sticker is literally the only thing about this house that isn't all old-ladified.

Well, that and the groggy teenager staring at it.

Carol isn't sleeping, either. I don't know what time she normally wakes up each morning, but no matter how early I drag myself out of bed (which is never very, if I can help it), she's always up and at 'em. Cooking, cleaning, grading papers, reading—the lady is never not doing something productive. I don't know how she does it.

But then again, even with the nightmares butting in, I feel like I've never slept better. I mean, it took a few days to let down my guard and trust that some drunk guy or tweaking junkie wasn't going to wander in and mess me up, but once I did, I was amazed at how much better I felt.

It's a wonder what more than three hours of crappy sleep does for the screwed-up teenage body.

I touch the gold base of the lamp to turn it off. Another surprisingly cool piece of old tech. Took me, like, ten minutes to figure out how to turn the thing on the first night I was here. Made me feel like an idiot. Darkness douses the room like a thick blanket. Out here away from all the city lights, the dark is real. Not that fake dark like in the city where the streetlights are always on and the ugly yellow glow sneaks in no matter what and makes it even harder to sleep than it already is with all the noise and worry and fear.

The only light I can see comes from the soft glow of Carol's lamp in the bedroom down the hall. I lay back and stare at the swirling shapes in the darkness near the ceiling. When I first got here, I slept for fourteen straight hours after I finally let myself relax. The bed was so soft, and the room was so cool, chilled by the humming air conditioner jutting out of the upstairs hallway window. It was the first night in forever that I didn't have to just lie there and stew in my own putrid sweat. When I finally woke up, Carol was down in the kitchen fixing lunch. Fresh homemade chicken salad sandwiches and the most amazing apple pie for dessert. She'd stayed home from work just so I could sleep in. I learned later that it was the first day she'd taken off in nearly ten years. We sat there in her sunny kitchen and just chowed down in awkward silence, neither of us knowing where to start or what to say to break in our new normal.

After, we went outside to the garden and picked green beans. She showed me how to find and pick the ones that were ready, and I just went to town. Something about the smell of the dirt and the green things and the fresh air and the feel of the sun on my back just felt...*right*. Before I knew it, I was crying, my tears splashing on the pile of beans in the basket. And beside me, Carol just went picking along in silence, not asking questions, not forcing me to talk about things I don't even know *how* to talk about. The silence was like a cozy blanket—just covering us in a layer of love with no awkwardness at all. A couple of times I caught glints of wet in her eyes.

After, we sat in rocking chairs on the porch, *snap-snap-snapping* beans and tossing the little silver strings into a pile until we had a million little juicy tidbits just waiting to be eaten.

By the time we were done, the sun was dipping low in the sky, splashing pinks and oranges all over the world. I don't know where the hours of that day went, but they were some of the best ones I can remember.

I'll never forget that smell—so green, so *alive*—for as long as I live.

We spent the twilight walking down the quiet road stuffing plastic grocery bags full of beans into neighbors' mailboxes. After that, she showed me how she cooks them, flavoring with bits of leftover ham and bacon. I ate so much I thought I'd be sick.

I went to bed that night feeling like a newborn, all confused and scared and happy and feeling loved all at the same time.

Just when my blinks are starting to get long, I hear a noise down the hall. A minor commotion in Carol's room—the squeal of hinges and the quiet thumps and scrapes of movement. Odd. I've had my sleep stolen by nightmares a few times lately, and she's always been quiet as a mouse after—except the rustle of turning pages as she sits and reads in her faded blue high-back chair.

I really, really don't want to be nosy, but curiosity gets the better of me. I slide out of bed and creep into the hall. The rough weave of the faux-Persian runner tickles the bottoms of my feet as I scoot along in stealth mode. As I get closer, the sound of wet sniffling takes shape and mingles with the other stealthy movement sounds. Carol's bedroom door is open a crack, and through it I can catch a little sliver of the room. I could probably see more if I got closer, but I don't want to get caught being a creeper.

She's sitting on the bed with her back to the door, her gray head bent downward. Her shoulders bob as she quietly sobs over something cradled in her arms. I can't see what it is, but there's this little wooden chest on the bed next to her.

Little cracks form in my heart and compete with the burning curiosity raging inside me. Real internal tug-of-war going on, here. My hand hovers over the doorknob. I want so desperately to go comfort her/see what's in the box.

Nope. Don't do it, Randi. If she wanted you to know, she'd tell you. If she needed you, she'd let you know.

But would she?

My hand drops to my side, and I take a step backward. I beat down the furious curiosity monster raging inside me. Last thing I want to do is break her trust. She's done so much for me. Don't want to repay her by being a sneaky looky-loo.

I take another step back, and the floorboard screams, sending out a billion decibels into the quiet little house.

Carol gasps and turns toward me.

We lock eyes.

CHAPTER 4

Before I can even think about what I'm doing, I'm running through the little front yard in my fuzzy PJs and bare feet. The last time I got caught trying to look into Mom's room I couldn't sit straight for a week. No freaking way I'm letting that happen again. Better to take my chances on the streets until she cools off or passes out and forgets.

I vault the porch steps like a startled deer, ready to take off into the darkness. My feet hit the dew-wet grass and slip. Next thing I know, I find myself staring up at a clear sky jam-packed with white sparkles and wondering where the heck I am.

Grass? Where did that come from?

Dewdrops seep through my clothes and give me instant chills. I sit up and shake my head, struggling to clear out the cobwebs and gain my bearings.

"Miranda!" calls an unfamiliar voice. I tense to spring again, but I stop myself. "What on earth are you doing?"

That voice. It sounds scared, not angry. And clear, not clouded by smoke and cheap gas station liquor. No murder at all to be heard in that voice.

Weird.

Don't trust it! You've been fooled before!

The patter of light footsteps heads toward me. My eyes turn toward the sound, but the bright house lights blind me. All I can see is a small, dark shape. My heart races.

Time to go.

My feet kick into high gear, but the stupid wet grass gets me again. My butt slams back down on the cold ground before I can get anywhere.

The dark shape comes closer. It reaches for me. Blood roars in my ears, blotting out the words the shadow is speaking to me. I scream and cover my face, bracing myself for the pain.

I flinch at the first touch, but instead of hurting me, the arms wrap me up in a warm, tight embrace. The comforting smell of lavender and clean laundry breaks through my panic and sends calming waves up through my nose to radiate through my whole body.

Words come back into focus.

"...come back to me, Miranda. Please." The voice is calm, but I can hear fear creeping into it. Still no anger. "It's me, dear. Carol. You're safe here with me."

Carol.

Soft, warm bed. Safe, clean, food, love.

I remember.

The panic rushes out of me like air from a popped balloon. I grab her and squeeze, burying my face in the front of her pink fuzzy robe. Tears pour out with body-shaking sobs. She rocks me back and forth like a baby, making these hissy shushing sounds.

"I—I'm sorry," I manage to squeeze out between boo-hoos. "Heard a sound in your bedroom. You caught me looking, and I got scared because Mom used to—"

"It's okay," she cuts me off. "I told you. You don't have to be afraid anymore. You're here with me now."

I nod, my head still buried in her front. "I know. It's just that—that you might have to remind me. A lot."

I feel her nod. "It's only been a month, Miranda. Be patient with yourself. You've been through more than I can imagine. It's going to take a while to—"

"But what if I don't have a while?" I peel my face away from her chest and lock eyes with her. Hers are dripping, too. "What if they come back tomorrow or the next day or the next day and take me—"

"Shhh." She pulls me back in while my words ebb away with a baby girl whimper. "I will do everything in my power to stop it. But we will worry about that if the time comes. For now, dear, we must enjoy every day for the good it brings. We can't let worry darken our horizons."

I nod. Tears and snot smear the front of her fuzzy robe, but she doesn't seem to care.

She stands, her arms still wrapped around me. I follow. "Now. Let's get off this damp ground before we catch our deaths out here."

I deposit myself on the deep living room sofa. It squishes in so far I almost get swallowed up. Carol bends with a groan and flicks a switch on this little fireplace thing with fake logs. I jolt as orange flames leap to life with a *whoosh*.

Pretty neat. Never seen anything like that before.

The fires dance around in neat little rows, giving off an instant comforting warmth. Carol pads out of the room, and while I hear her banging around in the kitchen, I just stare at those flames and get totally lost in them.

Warm. Kids and teachers complain about the chilly classrooms at school. But after you've shivered all through the night because the only little heater in your house is blazing behind a locked bedroom door that isn't yours—well, pretty much anything is better than that.

After all, all the schools around here are like, a billion years old or something, so what do you expect?

Anyway, being warm is one of those things a lot of people take for granted. You can complain about being a little chilly all you want, but until you spend an entire winter walking the streets in nothing but a t-shirt and a ratty hoodie and then going home to shiver your scrawny butt off all night long because some junkie made off with the blanket you stole from the lost and found, don't come whining to me.

But *this*. This is really something. I feel like I'm in one of those movies where the family sits around the fire at Christmas and drinks hot chocolate and munches on some sweet treat and just generally has a cozy, happy time full of all sorts of feel-goods.

God, I hope I'm still here at Christmas.

And that's got nothing to do with getting some stupid presents. It's my shot to get a taste of some kind of happy instead of sitting in my cold, dark craphole of a house silently hating the whole world because everyone else but me seems to be having a happy, cozy time.

I don't know how long I sit there hypnotized by the orange flickers, lost in the dingy corridors of my memories, but when Carol clears her throat to snap me out of it, I flinch like I've been shot or something. A little shake of my head clears the cobwebs. Carol smiles and holds out a steaming mug of something. I take it, cupping my hands around it, drinking in the warmth of it through my fingers. She sits down next to me, her shoulder grazing mine.

Warm. There it is again.

So good.

That fear tries to sneak in again, but I beat it back. No way I'm going to let my stupid brain ruin this moment.

I take a sip. Coffee. I hate coffee, can't stand the bitter, nasty stuff. Like drinking a cup of hot punishment.

But I swear to God, this disgusting stuff is so delicious in this moment right now.

A smile creeps across my exhausted face.

CHAPTER 5

On Monday mornings, the teacher parking lot looks like a field hospital from one of those old wars where the doctors cut off limbs left and right (amputation pun) and people died of antique-sounding *Oregon Trail* diseases like dysentery and cholera. Ms. Morris, the youngest teacher on staff, sits in her little Prius and dabs at her eyes. As I watch, she keeps half-opening the door and slamming it closed like she can't decide whether she wants to go work for a living or give it all up and live in a van down by the river.

I've seen the way kids my age act, and I can honestly say it wouldn't be a hard choice for me.

I'd choose the river hermit life over dealing with a bunch of me's any day.

And it doesn't help that Halloween is in just a few days and all us kids have been running around all hopped-up on candy and pre-holiday jitters.

If I thought it would help, I'd peck on her window and try to explain that all her kids acting crazy really has nothing to do with her. It's seriously not personal. I mean, we've got so many hormones and emotions and issues right now they're lucky we don't all spontaneously combust and burn the school down around us. It's not like we *want* to act crazy, but we just can't help ourselves.

Mr. Braswell is trying to get his kid, this chunky little sixth-grader, to get out of the car. He drives this beat-up old jalopy of a pickup truck, and the kid is planted in the passenger seat like a lump of doughy clay. He's got his arms crossed in that typical stubborn adolescent way. Done that myself, like, a billion times. When I get like that, I feel powerful and so completely and utterly *right* about whatever I'm being a stubborn butthole about. Usually something stupid.

And I'm almost always wrong.

But when I look at it from this side, it just looks like some dumb kid being a total brat. I'll try to remember that the next time I think I'm going to pull that move, but I won't hold my breath.

The dad is huffing and puffing and turning all red in the face. I swear his ears look like they're about to burst into flames, and the back of his hairy neck looks hot enough to fry eggs on. He's so mad he keeps almost-cursing, but every time he's about to fire off a bleep-bleep, he suddenly remembers where he is and looks around the parking lot with this guilty, embarrassed look on his face. When he does, all the eyes in the audience suddenly dip down into phone screens or zoom up to the wispy October clouds. I kind of feel bad for the guy, but the show is so good I wish someone had thought to bring some popcorn.

While the parenting battle is raging, Ms. Morris has summoned the courage to at least get one foot onto the pavement. Good for her. Better than I could do.

This fancy black SUV rolls into the spot next to us. It's this new teacher I don't know. A transfer from some place with a faraway-sounding name. But I've been stuck in this town my whole life, so she could be from the next school over or from across the globe and it would make no difference to me. When you've been trapped like I have, everywhere is foreign.

The speakers are blaring, and at first, I think she's jamming. Maybe getting herself pumped up with some pre-work tunes. But when the car comes to a stop, I realize she's having a heated conversation with someone. Her phone is hooked up to the car speakers, and the guy on the other end of the line is really going for it. I can't make out the words, but the harsh rumbles and thumps tell me he's not being very nice.

I'm very familiar with that language.

She tries to say something, but the voice gets louder and cuts her off with a machine gun-fast blast of hateful-sounding words. She jolts with each one like the sounds are cutting into her, and with each little jump, she sinks lower and lower in her seat. She tries one more time to pipe up and say something, but he ends the call, the little triple-beep serving as his farewell and "have a good day."

It destroys her. She buries her face in her hands and sobs, her shoulders shaking up and down with big old boo-hoos.

It is *not* a fun show to watch.

"That stupid, no-good son of a—"

"*Carol!*" I gasp, cutting her off before she can utter the first naughty word I've ever heard her say. I immediately regret it because I'd love to have that piece of ammo in my chamber for when she scolds me the next time I slip up and drift back to talking like Ugly Me.

She clears her throat and releases her grip on the steering wheel, then straightens herself. She pins me with a super serious look. "If that man were standing before me right now, I would give him more than a piece of my mind." Her sentence ends with a huff of angry air, and she slings herself out of the car and slams the door behind her with more force than I thought possible.

As I watch in stunned silence, she marches over to the crying lady's car and knocks on the window. The woman starts and does a real quick wipe at her eyes before she rolls the window down. Carol leans in real close and wraps the lady up in a big hug. The woman melts into her and the two of them share a wordless moment.

My eyes start to burn, threatening tears. I rip myself away from the spectacle. Don't want to start my Monday going in with a case of cryface. Been there, done that way too many times to count, and I'm seriously trying to turn over a new leaf now.

Carol is talking to the lady now, but she's using this low, cooing voice, so I can't make out what she's saying. I look back at Mr. Braswell and the kid. He's still sitting there like a statue, but Papa's starting to get this defeated look. He's not yelling—just kind of whisper-shouting through clenched teeth. His voice keeps cracking, and I can tell he's holding back tears.

Poor guy.

Meanwhile, Ms. Morris is at least outside her car, but she's just standing there leaning against it. She's got her eyes closed, and I can tell she's doing that yoga breathing thing to calm her nerves.

I guess I forget most of the time that teachers are people, too. Not like they fold up and fit inside the desks at night. They have bratty kids and money issues and butthole spouses and anxiety, too. And, for some of them, probably a lot worse than that.

They're just as screwed-up and hurting as us kids are.

Oh, man.

I almost get knocked over by a rush of guilt as I contemplate the hell I've given my teachers over the years.

Well, I can't fix everything, but I can at least help one person today.

I walk over and tap on Braswell's shoulder. He gives a surprised jolt and turns around. His eyes widen a little bit when he sees me, and I can tell he's getting ready to let me have it for lurking out back here in the teacher lot. But then he suddenly remembers, and his face relaxes.

Hey, can't blame him. I'm still caught off-guard when I look in the mirror sometimes or wake up in a soft, warm bed.

"Let me give it a shot, Coach Morris," I say. "I've kind of, you know, had some experience being a stubborn kid. I can speak the language." I shoot what I hope is a disarming smile his way.

He softens and deflates, returning my smile. "Sure thing, kiddo. Can't do any worse than I am." He clears his throat and drops his eyes to the dingy pavement. "Probably best I step back, anyway. Was just about to let my temper get the best of me."

"Trust me, Coach. I know all about that, too." I remember Coach Morris's meaty hand wrapped around my arm, dragging me to the office after I went nutso on the star quarterback when he called me a—well, a not-nice thing. "You know that."

I crack another smile. Feels awkward, and I hope I'm not making things weird. Smiling still feels like a foreign language to me, and it's kind of scary practicing all the new words I'm learning.

He chuckles. "That I do, kid." He looks around to make sure no one's listening. "But that knucklehead had it coming."

I reply with my own little chuckle just to keep the good vibes flowing. I'm not so sure about that one, though. I mean, sure, the guy was a total jerk to call me that, but every time Ugly Me pays me a visit and I lose it on someone, I'm just left feeling sick and empty after. Hurting someone has never made me feel better about anything. It's just the only thing I ever knew how to do.

The kid's still sitting all cross-armed and mad when I lean into the truck. It's got that signature old truck smell—dust and grease and sun-cracked vinyl. Dad tries to creep closer to hear what I'm going to say, but I wave him off.

"You know what would really piss your dad off?" I try on a devious smile, size five.

His face softens, and his green eyes flit over to meet mine for a split second. He's listening.

"So he's been yelling and screaming for a while now. Really going for it, you know?"

A little shadow of a grin cracks the corner of his dead-set mouth.

"What if you just, you know, walked in after this little conversation? Show him what all his yelling and dad stuff gets him?" I give him a little nudge with my elbow.

The reluctant little smile spreads to the other corner.

"Imagine how crazy it'll drive him that some kid could do something he couldn't." I give him another nudge. "I mean, his head might, like, actually explode or something."

He looks at me and nods, one little curt gesture. I step back, and the kid snatches up his backpack, jumps down out of the truck, and jogs to the door. On the way, he starts this big, fake belly laugh. I guess he decided to add his own touch to the show. Not bad. Coach's hackles rise again. Another teacher lets the kid in, shooting a bewildered look back our way.

"Don't sweat it," I say, trying to quell the new heat rising. "When we do stuff like that, we're just trying to get under your skin. It's nothing personal. If you act like it doesn't make you want to rip our heads off, we start to lose interest pretty quick."

He looks down at me with a raised eyebrow.

"Short attention spans, you know?" I shrug. "Plus, I know what I'm talking about. Got a master's degree in crazy adolescent studies."

He chuckles, and the red sheen on the back of his neck goes to a blotchy white.

As I walk into the school, I feel an unfamiliar sensation taking over me.

Did it just feel really good to help someone, or am I really losing it?

That good feeling lasts for an entire thirty seconds before I get to class and see the partner assignments for the new group project.

CHAPTER 6

Phoebe Matson.

AKA Headband Girl.

Of all the horrible people in all the horrible corners of this horrible world.

Her.

I rub my eyes, really digging in until specks of light dance around in the dark behind my closed eyelids. I snap them open, hoping the words on the board have somehow changed, that my sleepy eyes were mistaken or something.

Nope. There it is in writing up on the whiteboard.

Miranda Lewis and Phoebe Matson: Leaves

Does he seriously expect me to work with *her?*

For a split-second, it crosses my mind to run up to the board and erase the whole thing and pray that Mr. Worsham gets mad enough at me to forget who he partnered with who. But then it occurs to me that the list is a projection. Stupid modern technology ruining my stupid life.

Wonder if I can bribe one of the computer geeks into hacking Mr. Worsham's computer? I mean, getting out of working with her is definitely worth committing a felony, right?

The chatter of the students shuffling into the classroom fades out behind the whine of blood rushing to my head.

I turn away from the board in a panicked daze. The projector light shines in my eyes and blinds me to all the faces around me. I stare up at the blazing bulb. Maybe I can roast my retinas, get out of this thing for medical reasons. Or get a doctor's note from some quack.

"Oh. My. *God*." The voice is unmistakably *hers*. Stupid whiny, nasaly noise. I'd rather listen to a string of wet dog farts. She sounds almost as happy about this turn of events as I am.

We may hate each other's guts, but at least we can agree on something.

Her cronies give off a chorus of laughter. She silences them with a hiss.

Without missing a beat, she clears her throat and turns on the charm. She uses her suck-up, talking-to-adults voice, which is even more annoying than her normal one. "Um, Mr. Worsham, sir. May I speak with you about the project assignments, please?"

I spin toward the sound, ready to join forces with the Evil One for just long enough to get out of this mess. My foot catches on the leg of a desk, and I go sprawling in a big, messy tangle of limbs and classroom furniture. By the time the dust settles, I'm sporting, like, a hundred different little pains, and the loudest silence ever has taken over the classroom.

Mr. Worsham utters this little choking sound and rushes over, shoving kids away left and right. They fly through the air like leaves in a windstorm. I'd be totally impressed if I wasn't suffering an excruciating case of embarrassment right now.

A murmur of giggles is rippling through the classroom when Mr. Worsham's head pops into my field of vision, obstructing my view of the ceiling. His face is all red, and his gross combover hair is dislodged. It hangs so low it brushes the tip of my nose.

Ick.

"Somebody get the nurse!" he yells, his twangy voice cracking as it rises into the stratosphere. I can feel/smell his coffee breath on my face.

Double ick.

I start to rise, but he gently presses me back to the floor.

His face is super serious, and his red is fading into a sickly green. "Lie still, Miss Lewis. It's important in the case of a head inj—"

I brush his hand away and sit up. "I'm okay, Mr. Worsham. Really. I didn't even hit my head. I'm just clumsy, is all."

The laughter dancing around in the air intensifies. Mr. Worsham ignores it. I wish I could ignore it, but it burns into my head like one of those red-hot poker things they use on those poor cows on TV.

"Now, Ms. Lewis," he says, his voice drowning in the laughter. "I insist. You must visit the school nurse after a fall like that. Just to be safe."

Heat blazes in my cheeks. If I concentrate hard enough, could I just melt into the floor? That would be better than standing up and facing all these smirking faces.

But no such luck.

Someone at the door clears her throat in that "I mean serious business way." The room quiets down in a hurry.

It's the school nurse. And she's not alone.

She's got the rickety old school wheelchair with her.

You've got to be kidding me. A freaking *wheelchair*?

I utter a curse under my breath. Mr. Worsham's eyes flick down at me, but he doesn't say anything.

Oops. There goes Ugly Me again.

All eyes are on me as Mr. Worsham and the nurse half-drag, half-lift me into the wheelchair. I could get up and walk, but I'm paralyzed by the thick layer of shamesauce covering my entire being.

The silence is worse than the laughter.

The nurse wheels me out. Meanwhile, the dams are bursting at the seams with pent-up laughter.

It finally lets loose when I'm a few feet out of the doorway.

I wish I would have broken my neck, but I'm just not that lucky.

CHAPTER 7

By the time I'm finally able to free myself from the nurse's clutches, science class is over. I rush upstairs, digging in my backpack for last night's homework. I could probably turn it in tomorrow, but I'm lucky to have kept up with it this long.

I freeze when I realize what I'm doing.

I still can't get used to the feeling of, you know, actually doing what I'm supposed to. Back in the before times, I'd have milked this whole falling down thing for all it was worth. Probably would have hung around in the nurse's office all day long with everyone googooing and gagaing all over me and bringing me snacks and generally just making a big old messy fuss.

Funny how that not being a total miserable, half-starved sad sack has a way of changing, like, *everything*. I mean, one minute I'm walking around hating the world and wanting to fight everyone who looks at me sideways, and the next I'm fast-limping up a flight of stairs to turn in my homework. *Completed* homework, that is.

I mean, I'm still mess of scars and fears, but it's crazy the wonders a warm bed and a belly full of food will do for a girl.

When I first got to Carol's, my grades were in the dumps. Below the dumps, actually. In a hundred-foot-deep pit. With rusty spikes at the bottom. But after a few days of not being in total survival mode constantly, something weird happened.

I started to care about stuff. Stuff I thought was stupid before. Stuff like grades and homework and not being a total turd to everyone all the time. I saw everything like it was shiny and new, glistening with fresh details I'd never noticed before. Like sometimes when you're watching a YouTube video on a bad connection. The first part is all fuzzy and gross before it catches up to itself and becomes crispy clear.

To be honest, it kind of freaked me out at first. I felt like an alien who crashed on a planet filled with people who happened to look like me, but I had no idea how to act to blend in. I stumbled around all blind and disoriented, hoping desperately I wouldn't get found out as an imposter and get sent back to my home planet in the Crapatron Galaxy.

I'd turned over a new leaf, but I no longer recognized the tree.

But after a few days of actually trying, I settled into a place that actually felt...*good*. And that freaked me out, too. My grades started to climb, and for the first time in my life, I felt successful. I was able to finally chalk up a "W" for Miranda. I'd been so used to losing that I had no idea how it felt to win one.

All because of Carol, the one person I thought hated my stinking guts the most turned out to be, like, the best person in the world.

I guess that goes to show you may *think* you know someone only to turn around and get your whole world rocked.

Someone grabs the back of my arm and jerks me free from my daydream. I snap back to reality and go into immediate defense mode, ready to strike with fangs and claws and rip faces off. This little growl escapes me before

I know what's happening. I catch myself with my fist cocked and ready to fly.

Hey, it's only been a month. Some habits die hard.

"*Jesus*, psycho! Take it easy!" Headband Girl releases my arm and takes a step backward, a startled expression spread across her too-rosy cheeks. I can practically smell the bubblegum she's always chaw-chawing on with her stupid, crap-spewing mouth.

My blood boils. For half a second, I contemplate just going ahead and slugging her. If I didn't have Carol counting on me not being a certifiable nutcase anymore, I'd probably go ahead and do it.

But now that I've got something to live for, this is *so* not worth it.

My fist unclenches, but I stay on high alert. "Ugh. What do *you* want?"

She rolls her eyes and makes a noise like something's caught in the back of her throat. "We gotta go see Mr. Worsham. There's no freaking way I'm gonna work with you on this project, and I know you feel the same. We gotta convince him to let us switch partners."

Gag. But I guess she's right. Suppose I'll have to join forces with The Evil One just this once, for everyone's good.

"Fine. As much as I hate to admit it, you're right. I'd rather work with a sackful of rabid raccoons than spend a second working with you."

Dang. That was mean. I almost regret coming back at her like that. I mean, aren't I supposed to be better than this?

Baby steps, I suppose.

She rolls her eyes again and pops the giant wad of pink gum. For half-a-second, I swear there's this little hurt look that flashes across her face, but I decide not to pour too much thought into that. "Whatever. Let's just get this over with," she says through the mouthful of pink stuff.

A bunch of sixth-graders are filing into Mr. Worsham's class when we get there. We duck our heads in, but he's nowhere to be seen. The scene is a total war zone. One kid is dancing in the corner of the room. Some kind of dance from a video game, I think. He's not very good at it. He thinks he looks cool, but he just looks like a big dork. Another one is just spinning around in place making these high-pitched meowing sounds over and over. One girl is dragging some poor boy across the floor by his backpack.

Holy crap. What is wrong with these kids? Did I act like that during my first stint in sixth grade?

No. I was too busy being suspended for half the year for fighting and skipping class.

Headband Girl and I share a look. Probably the first non-"I hate you" period of eye contact we've ever had. This one says, "These kids are freaking lunatics."

The two of us jump when someone clears their throat loudly behind us. The zoo falls into quick order, chairs scraping on the floor as the kids rush to settle in. It's almost like they think that if they move fast enough, he won't have noticed what a bunch of hellions they were being just a second ago when he walked in and saw them.

"May I help you ladies?" Mr. Worsham asks.

We share another look, this one a tug of war where the loser has to talk first.

I lose.

"Um, we were just—uh—well, we were—um—"

Oh, my God. It's as if I've never spoken English before.

Headband Girl to the rescue. "Mr. Worsham, sir," she says in her thickest sticky-sweet talking-to-adults-while-trying-to-hide-her-true-evil-nature-filled voice. "Miranda and I are requesting a change of partners for the project, sir." She doesn't wait for him to chime in—just charges on full force. "You see, she and I have a personality conflict. You may remember the incident a few weeks ago. Well, in light of that, we both believe it's best if—"

He holds up his hand to cut her off. She zips it quick.

Cool trick. Wish I could do that.

"I'm afraid that's not possible, ladies." His spectacled eyes flit between us, then down the hallway. Something down there among the tangle of awkward bodies catches his eye. He clears his throat and snaps his attention back to us. "Perhaps you can put your differences aside for the duration of the project. The two of you are smart young ladies. I'm confident you can figure something out."

At this, he shuffles past us and walks into his classroom.

I try to pipe up, but a slamming door cuts me off mid-word. I'm left standing there fishmouthing, choking on whiny the words I didn't get to say.

"*Great*," Headband Girl spits, her voice full of poison. She punctuates the word with a little fussy stomp.

Well, back to reality. Sweet-talking girl sure didn't last long.

I turn toward my next class, totally prepared to wallow in defeat. She grips my arm again.

Her face is firm, tinged with red. She's building up into a real tizzy. "Where are you going? Just because that old coot won't let us switch doesn't mean it's over."

I growl and jerk my arm free. "Um, I think it kind of does." I can feel the fire rising in my voice.

Careful now. Don't need Ugly Me to make an unwelcome reappearance over this. So not worth it.

She rolls her stupid eyes at me. Adults tell little kids if they do that their face will get stuck that way.

I wonder what happened to my face, then.

She nods her head toward the stairwell. "Come with me down to the office. We'll complain to the principal."

My turn to roll my eyes. This is so stupid. I've spent enough time in the office to get an idea of all the crap they have to deal with. No freaking way I'm going down there to whine about this.

She starts walking away, so I use her own arm-grabby move against her. She spins to face me. A wisp of hair comes loose and dangles in her face like a birthday party streamer.

"Listen, maybe it's best we just get this over with. We don't need to—"

"*Ladies*," Carol's sharp voice cuts through. We both start like we've been caught at some kind of dirty deed.

She's standing behind us, her hands on her hips in that "I mean business" way. "A word, please."

Headband Girl and I share a silent "oh crap" look.

"Y—yes, ma'am," HG squeaks out. Her voice has lost all its confident sweetness.

I look down at the floor.

Carol clears her throat. "Now the two of you wouldn't be trying to get out of this group project, would you?"

I pretend to study a particularly interesting dust bunny. Headband Girl shifts from foot to foot like she's standing on a bed of nails.

She sees the guilt plastered all over us like two teenage billboards.

"That's what I thought." She takes a step closer. For such a small lady, she sure knows how to be menacing. Must have taken a class in college or something.

HG gets a sudden rush of courage. "Ms. Odum, you know what happen—"

Carol silences her with a razor-sharp glance. HG's eyes dart downward. "I know full well what happened, young lady. And that little childish incident does not serve as an excuse for the two of you to weasel out of this project."

I decide to pipe up. "But that's so stup—"

I immediately regret my decision to open my idiotic, fat mouth when Carol shoots me a fully loaded "wait until we get home" look.

"The two of you will put your petty differences aside and complete this project as assigned. And if you have anything else to say about your partnership, you can address those comments to me."

My eyebrow goes full cock, shooting toward the ceiling.

"Because *I'm* the one who requested that the two of you work together."

CHAPTER 8

"But she's nothing but a spoiled rich kid, that's why!"

Carol sighs and shakes her head over the steaming pot of boiling water. It's spaghetti night, pretty much my favorite. She uses this homemade pasta sauce she makes from her garden veggies and preserves in these cool glass jars she keeps lined up in neat rows down in the cellar. After I first moved in, I'd just go down there and stare at all the jars, my mouth watering the whole time thinking about all the homegrown food she packed in them all by herself. Must have taken hours and hours and hours to do it all. She's got enough food down there to last for, like, ever.

Carol calls it "canning," even though the food goes into those glass jars. Should be called "jarring," but that somehow sounds weirder. She promised to teach me how to do it later this fall when she makes applesauce from the fruit on tree in her backyard. They're these tiny rock-hard things that taste like sour garbage when you bite them but somehow make amazing applesauce.

I'm pretty pumped about learning how to do that, but I'm trying not to get my hopes up too much in case someone swoops in to take me back to my old life.

Dinner smells amazing, but I've lost my appetite tonight. Not even the delicious smells wafting out of the kitchen are enough to break me out of this funk. I stomp out of the kitchen like a brat and post up by the front windows. She's twenty minutes late already, and I'm hoping that means she's not going to show at all.

"It is time that you learned that the simple presence of money does not make for a better life." I hear a whoosh of water and steam as she dumps the pot into the beat-up colander that belonged to her mother. "You have lived a life no child should have to, but despite what you may think, there are other children in the world who suffer as well. You need to learn to see beyond simple appearances and your own biased assumptions."

Yeah, yeah. Blah, blah, blah. I don't see how doing some stupid project with a girl I hate is going to somehow change my life, but whatever. I'm just ready to get it over with and get on with my life.

I'm working up some kind of smart-alecky response, but the rumble of an engine outside shatters my concentration. This shiny black BMW car rolls to a stop in the middle of the road in front of the house. There's this pretty, youngish-looking woman in the driver's seat. She's all done up in a thick layer of makeup and wears this tiny black dress that reveals way too much of what's up top. I'm not sure where this lady is headed, but she sure looks like she's after something, if you know what I mean.

The car sits there for a second while HG and her mystery chauffeur talk. I can't hear what they're saying, of course, but driver's head is bobbing and weaving like a boxer's while HG sinks lower and lower into her seat with each word. Definitely not a nice conversation.

Been there, done that.

Eventually, HG gets out of the car and slams the door. Her face is all red and flushed, and she dabs at the corners of her eyes. The car doesn't even wait for her to cross over onto Carol's front walk before it speeds away.

Good freaking thing she was at the right house or God knows whose door she'd be knocking on. HG has to take a quick step back to avoid having her toes squished. Her foot catches on something in the ditch, and she goes tumbling backward onto her butt. After the dust settles, she just kind of sits there for a second like a lost puppy, looking around all scared and uncertain. Tears flow freely down her cheeks now.

And suddenly it's like I'm seeing a whole new girl. The rich, spoiled, popular brat is gone, her costume left behind in that speeding car. All that's left is a kind of someone who looks all too familiar.

"Don't just sit there like a lump of clay." I jump as Carol's sharp scold shatters my contemplative moment. "Go greet her."

She's standing there on the other side of the road when I open the door. We study each other like we're both discovering a new species, neither one of us talking—just sort of standing there and staring at each other, locked in some sort of awkward trance. Carol breaks the spell by sneaking up behind me and shouting out into the street. I jump, like, a million miles into the air.

"Well, don't just stand there! Come on in, Ms. Matson!"

HG's eyes go wide when her brain registers the fact that she's been dumped off at none other than the meanest teacher in school's front door. That makes a little smile blossom on my face. I remember those days back when I thought Carol was a giant, fire-breathing, rhymes-with-"itch."

But now that I've seen past her pain, I've got a whole new perspective.

Carol turns and heads back to the kitchen, leaving me alone with HG. Her mouth is hanging open now. A giant wad of pink bubblegum flops out and disappears into the scrubby roadside grass at her feet.

Before I can stop it, a giggle sneaks its way out. "Well, come on before you get squashed by a truck or something."

She snaps to attention with a little head wiggle and slams her mouth closed. Her chest rises with a deep inhalation as she screws up her courage to enter the belly of the beast and go behind closed doors with crabby old Odum and Dumpster Girl.

She must think it's some kind of set-up. Can't say I blame her.

She pauses at the foot of the little brick steps leading up to the front porch. Her Adam's apple takes a trip up and down her throat before she begins to climb. She wipes at a fresh tear welling up in the corner of her eye.

By the time she gets to the front door, she's shaking.

CHAPTER 9

Phoebe scans the bedroom, her eyes taking in all the new old stuff. "Um, so Ms. Odum is, like, your—"

"Foster mom, I guess you could say." I've never really thought about that before, so I'm surprised how quick the answer comes to me. I click the door closed behind us to shut out the cooking smells. No way I'm going to be able to concentrate if my stomach is screaming for food the whole time.

I lived a lot of my life that way. Trying to concentrate on school when all you can really think about is getting something to eat is a unique type of torture. I swear I've been so hungry before that I couldn't add two and two. Literally.

She gives the closed door a nervous glance. Thin pink streaks of new skin glisten on the side of her face. My heart does a guilty somersault.

"You can relax, you know. I'm not going to try to rip your face off again or anything like that."

Her hand darts toward her cheek, but she catches it halfway. She gives me a wary quarter-smile.

My eyes hit the carpet. "Sorry about that, by the way. I had some, um, stuff going on."

I almost gag on the words, but it kind of feels good to say them.

She's as surprised as I am. "Oh. Um, it's—it's okay." She digs the toe of one of her sequiny flats into the carpet like a shy cartoon girl. "I—uh...I think I kind of deserved it, maybe. I mean, I acted like such a bit—"

I clear my throat to cut her off. We may be behind closed doors, but Carol's got the hearing of...of whatever kind of animal has really, really good hearing. Too much buzzing around in my head to make a good animal simile. No wordy-dirds allowed in this house. Learned that one the hard way. Still struggle with it, actually. But in my defense, I grew up in a bilingual household—English and profanity. I didn't realize it until Carol took me in, but the more you hear something, the more you say it. And the more you say it, the harder it is to stop saying it when you need to.

"But yeah," I say, breaking the awkward silence. "You were. A *huge* one. Like, monumental." Her face goes pink, and she looks down. "But that didn't mean you deserved what I did to you. I don't want to be that girl. Not anymore."

She nods, and her eyes rise to meet mine. They're still red from crying outside. "So what happened?"

I plop down on the bed. The old springs squeal with the sudden weight. "What do you mean?"

She deposits herself onto the little floral-print sofa across the room. "Like, *you know*. Why are you *here*?" She waves her hand around the room.

I lie back and pretend to stargaze through the ceiling. I take on a dreamy voice. "Why are any of us here? What is our purpose in life?" I'm not necessarily trying to be a smart-A—I'm just stalling while I decide if I want to actually talk about this or not.

Phoebe rolls her eyes and softens just a bit. "You know what I mean. If you don't want to answer, you can just say so."

A new silence creeps its way in. I'm thankful for the way out. Do I want to tell her? Do I even trust her? I mean, I know I felt bad for her after her sister or whoever dumped her here like a sack of hot garbage, but has anything really changed between us? Prickly memories tumble around inside my mind.

Dumpster Girl. Trash. What smells?

These memories claw at my brain, trying to stir up a dormant anger, trying to activate the Ugly Me that still lives deep inside. Though she hasn't made an appearance since the day I moved in with Carol.

No. If I'm turning over a new leaf here, I want it to be fresh, green. Not some old dried-up dead one.

"Long, sad story," I say, tracing the pattern of some kind of blue flower on the bedspread. "But the gist of it is that my folks got hooked on drugs, and now they're both locked up."

She nods and releases a big sigh. "That sucks."

"Yep."

Good talk. Now time to change the subject.

"So who was that who dropped you off? Your older sister?"

She snorts, not a laughy one, but a disgusted sound. "Nope. That would be my mom."

My mouth drops open. "Seriously? She looks like—"

"Yeah, I know," she cuts me off with a wicked eye roll. "She looks like a college kid. Acts like one, too."

I think that sounds kind of fun, but from the look on her face, she thinks very differently. "So I take it that's a problem? I mean, seems like it'd be fun."

"Yeah." She looks at the carpet and shakes her head. "It *might* be fun if she spent any of that time on me instead of on chasing the next in her long line of scummy guys." She grabs up a pillow and squeezes it tight against her chest. "That's where she was in such a hurry to get to tonight. Party at some dude's lake house. She got, like, super mad because bringing me all the way out here made her late for it."

"Oh." Profound, I know, but I can't think of anything else to say. I'm still kind of freaked out by all this. So used to hating her, it feels weird to feel bad for her.

"'Oh' is right." She tosses the pillow back onto the sofa and clears her throat. "So are we ready to do this?"

The abrupt segue is music to my ears. I mean, I'm fine to not absolutely hate her guts anymore or to not actively want to murder her, but I'm not ready to walk hand-in-hand into the sunset, and I get the sense she isn't, either.

But the weight of that burning pile of hatred is gone from my heart, and it feels good.

We go into school mode for a while and knock out the project. Along the way, we share some light chitchat *yada yada*, but we mostly focus on the work. The project's really not that big of a deal, just a neon green poster board decorated with drawings of leaves and "fun facts," which, if I'm being honest, are actually more fun than I care to admit.

Weird.

I guess now that I'm not in perpetual survival mode, I can actually enjoy things like this.

Before, I wouldn't have even done the thing. Even if I would've had the mental and emotional capacity to care about a school project, the likelihood of getting the poster board and markers would have been smaller than a tick turd. And all the creativity I could have mustered—which would have been next to none—would have been poured into finding an excuse that would have a snowball's chance in Hades of holding up in the court of school.

Turns out Headband Gir—Phoebe is a pretty darn good artist, and when her drawings are combined with my lists of facts, a not-half-bad project materializes. I hang it up on the wall with a couple pieces of tape, and we stand back to admire our work.

Phoebe crosses her arms and nods. "Well, what do you think?"

When I look at the thing, I get this weird feeling in my chest. At first, I almost panic because I think I'm having an aneurysm or something, but with a little work, I'm able to pinpoint it.

I'm actually kind-of, sort-of proud.

For the first time I can remember, I actually feel good about something I've done. My eyes start to burn. I'm used to being a perpetual failure, a half-asleep, invisible observer of the goings-on of normal kids. An excuse-making machine quietly making straight F's in the background. Biding my time until I can just fade into the nothing of a crappy life and live happily never after. I didn't really want to not care, but after so much pretending like I didn't give half a crap about all the failing grades and eye rolls from teachers, I just kind of went numb. I never totally didn't care, but I gave up trying because it never seemed to matter.

I mean, I was too busy just surviving to find the time or mental steam to do all the homework thrown at me every day, so it really didn't matter how hard I worked at school because I was going to fail, anyway.

But *this*. This feels good. To know I'll be walking into class with something other than a lame excuse or a fake "I don't give a crap" shrug—well, it's nice.

I clear my throat, trying to play it cool. "Um." My voice threatens to break up. Another phlegmy throat clear. "I think it looks pretty good. What about you?"

She steps forward and smooths the curled-up corner. She crosses her arms and frowns at the poster. She tilts her head and makes a disapproving sound. I bite my lip and study her face, terrified of what she's going to say next, waiting for her to shatter my newfound feel-good.

She looks at me, her frown melting upward into a grin.

"I think we make a surprisingly good team."

CHAPTER 10

D inner was amazing. Tasted even better than it smelled. We ate a lot and chatted a little, with Carol making sure there weren't too many awkward silences. She filled those with stories about her own childhood growing up on a farm with her mom and sisters. Ha! Knew it! Sounded almost like some kind of *Little House on the Prairie* setup, except her Pa had died on some faraway battlefield. Not a penny to their name, but lots of love and good times and innocent shenanigans to go around. No Internet constantly feeding her lies about what's cool or normal. No social media spitting out hate and hurt all the time.

Sounds pretty good to me.

Maybe our science project should have been to build a time machine.

My favorite story was about this rooster named Ricky. He was this tiny little scrap of a thing with a huge, nasty attitude and an even bigger mouth.

Sounds like someone I used to know.

It's clear Phoebe's mom isn't coming to get her when 9:00 rolls around. She's spent the last hour and a half glued to the front windows making, like, a billion unanswered calls and constantly checking her phone. Hasn't spoken at all in the last half hour, just sitting there like a little doggy waiting for its owner to come home while me and Carol go about our nightly routine, tiptoeing around her situation. Each time the yellow glow of approaching headlights illuminates the front windows, she perks up and her ponytail bobs in this hopeful way. But when the bright glow fades to red as the cars pass, she deflates. It's excruciating to watch.

Some small leftover mean part of me wants to fault her for continuing to keep her hopes up for so long, but then a sudden memory bobs up from the depths of my nearly forgotten memories.

A little me waiting by the window of some random neighbor's house. Mom promising her she'd be back before lunch—maybe an hour, tops. Just have to run and get some groceries is all. Flashing a painted-on, "you know how it is" smile. The house smelled like cats. Not in a bad way, though. Things were tidy and clean, but a faint litterbox scent still hung around the air. Not much you can do about that.

The hour went by fast with me running around the house with the cats. Three of them. The lady had this little bright yellow feather tied to the end of a string, and the little beasties went nuts over it. Especially this chunker of a tabby named Roscoe. My giggles made me forget I'd been dumped at a stranger's house like a sack of old potatoes. But when the exhausted cats disappeared to their hidey holes to recover, I took my post at the front windows. There was this old patchwork quilt draped across the back of the sofa, and I leaned on it, my cheek pressed against it and my knees resting on the threadbare cushion. I traced the patterns with my little fingers, my ears tuned to the sound of approaching vehicles.

Time passed, and no matter how many cars passed and kept on going, the same little rush of hope stirred in me every time I heard the low rumble of an engine. And every time it wasn't her, that little hope died, leaving behind a little scar that got deeper and deeper. Eventually, I watched for headlights in the gathering darkness, that little hope rising and crashing down each time.

I woke up to the sound of angry words. Curled up on the sofa, wrapped up in the quilt with Roscoe sleeping warm and cozy in the crook behind my legs like a purring engine. Don't remember the words, but the lady wasn't happy with my mom. Mom picking some lame excuse from her list and giving a fake apology. Probably mustered up enough tears to convince the lady not to call social services.

She was good at that.

On the way home, the clock on the car stereo told me it was almost midnight.

I'm standing in the doorway of the living room with an armload of my dirty laundry studying the back of her head when it suddenly hits me that I'm here feeling for Phoebe all over again. My heart is stirring for a girl I hated a few hours ago, for a girl I used to swear was nothing but a rich, stuck-up, popular snob.

I used to think I was the only kid walking around school with issues, was the only one with secret pains that ate at me all day long until I was nothing more than a walking, talking collection of scars. But is it possible we're all like that? That we're all hurting, that we all have a story illustrated with pain? I think of Carol, no longer simply a grumpy old bat of a teacher, but actually a nice human being living with the constant ache of loss. The picture of her late husband on her desk at work. The box hidden away in her room. I think of Phoebe, no longer reduced to just being the Headband Girl caricature of a rich brat, but a little girl wanting her mother to care about her half as much as she cares about living it up with the next random guy who'll give her the time of day.

Is it possible that we're all blinded by our own pain, unable—or unwilling—to see the pain of everyone around us? I mean, I was always so focused on my own problems that I couldn't see anyone else's. I just assumed I was the only one and pretty much hated everyone else for not being miserable like me.

If we all took the time to really see other people—and I mean really, really *see* them—how much better off would we all be?

I think of all the ugly looks, the hateful words. How many of those were launched my way without anyone ever thinking there was more to me than what they saw or heard or smelled? How many of them stopped to consider that maybe I wasn't really the *bad kid* they thought I was? That maybe I was the *hurting kid*? That maybe I needed a cheeseburger and a nice word more than I needed detention?

And the same goes for me. How many times has something I did or said made an already hurting person hurt that much more? That maybe the jerk who called me "Dumpster Girl" needed a hug more than they needed a punch to the nose?

I drop my laundry and start forward, ready to say something to Phoebe, even though I'm not sure how to say what I want to say.

But the jingle of keys stops me in my tracks. I look back to see Carol. She's dressed in her nightgown, but she's got her purse and keys.

She gives them a jingle, a sad expression set in her face. I nod.

CHAPTER 11

C arol tapes a note to the front door on the way out just in case Phoebe's mom happens to actually come by while we're taking her home. I offer Phoebe shotgun, but she plops herself down in the back seat. She rides with her arms crossed over her chest and her forehead resting on the window. Carol tries to engage her in some small talk, but her monosyllabic answers communicate that she's not in the mood.

The car slides along filled with tense, sleepy silence. Carol seems to know where she's going, but once we pass out of the other side of the city, I'm totally lost. I learned pretty early on that kids like me don't belong on this side of the tracks, so I never roamed out here. Rows and rows of well-kept houses roll past, their mostly dark interiors lit in the bluish glow of televisions. No real mansions out here—just reasonable-sized houses—but compared to where I grew up, this may as well be Bel Air. No junked-out cars, no loose garbage, no aimless drifters in sight. The air isn't polluted with the smoke of a thousand cigarettes and other things. A few yoga pants-wearing moms and dudes with dad bods are out walking dogs or taking nighttime jogs, but otherwise, the whole place is bathed in a calm buzz of sleepy activity.

But what catches my eye more than anything are the decorations. Every house we pass is done up for the Halloween season in some way or another. There's at least one jack-o'-lantern on each stoop and front porch casting their glowing grins out into the night. Some houses have cutesy scenes with smiling scarecrows and tall stands of dried cornstalks and bales of straw. "Happy Fall, Y'all!" My favorites, though, are the ones who have taken out all the stops and have turned their little front lawns into outdoor houses of horror. Wooden tombstones with silly, punny names (Ted N. Buried, Ima Goner, Barry A. Live), grinning skeletons, dark figures suspended from tree limbs swaying in the wind, ghosts, bats, werewolf statues with glowing eyes.

The whole place is amazing.

Before all the bad started happening, Halloween was my favorite holiday. The memories are distant and fuzzy, obscured by all the pain and bullcrap I've been through. But they're still there. Carving a pumpkin with mom, giggling the whole time because pulling out the seeds and gunk made her gag. We bought them from on top of this dusty old farm wagon parked outside this church in our old neighborhood. She gave it the real college try because I couldn't wait for Dad to get home from work. But she eventually made a dash for the restroom while I collapsed with little kid laughter. Literal rolling on the floor laughing.

Dad coming home and lifting me up like he always did, me telling him about Mom losing her lunch and us laughing about it together. He finished the whole thing up lickety-split. It smiled at me with a half-crooked smile set under triangle-ish eyes spaced too far apart. I didn't care that it wasn't a perfect picture book jack-o'-lantern. It was perfect to me because it was ours. That night they had to carry me inside because I fell asleep in the front yard just staring at the flickering light dancing inside our pumpkin.

A few days later, I was Daddy's princess, so pretty in a pink floofy dress with a plastic tiara pinned in my hair. We held hands going door to door, giggling and laughing like three happy kids, our sounds mingling with the other families' until the whole city seemed to come alive with the music of joy. I came back with so much candy in my pillowcase that I didn't finish it until Easter, but what I savored most was the feeling of my hands in theirs, the feeling of weightless bliss as they'd *one-two-three* lift me up by my little arms to float between them.

A smile creeps across my lips as my eyes flit across a jack-o'-lantern with a wickedly crooked set of teeth.

I don't know when that Halloween was, but it's the last one I remember. After that, Halloween was just another thing to remind me of what I'd lost. It was just another thing that I couldn't be a part of, another thing that made me hate all the people who weren't like me, who had parents who made costumes and carved pumpkins and held hands giggling and laughing down the sidewalk.

But I don't know. I don't hate this.

Something about this time feels different. I can't put my finger on it. Maybe it's having a belly full of home-cooked food. Maybe it's knowing I'm not going to have to worry about random weird guys in my house tonight. Maybe it's riding shotgun next to someone who gives a crap about me.

Maybe it's knowing that I'm not the only one in the universe with a few messed-up chapters in her story.

But this time feels different. Last year, I'd see all these perfectly imperfect houses and their cheesy decorations and melt into a stewing pot of jealous hate for sure. It would have put me on the fast track for some big time Ugly Me. But something about this, this new, brighter *right here, right now* makes me able to see all this in a new light.

Before I can stop myself, words spew forth. "Can we get some pump-kins, Carol?"

She gives me a surprised side-eye.

I immediately feel guilty for asking. She's already done so much for me. More than she could ever know.

I clear my throat. "But it's okay if we can't. I just thought it might be fun to, you know, carve some jack-o'-lanterns. Haven't done that in ages."

My face burns a deep shade of red. Good thing it's dark in here.

"I would absolutely love that, Miranda." A smile perks up the corner of her mouth.

She turns into the driveway of a medium-ish house. It's one of those types where one part of the house is higher than the other. The type that when you walk in you immediately have to choose whether to go up or down some stairs. Makes me tired just thinking about climbing all those stairs all the time. It's the only house on the block not all done up for the season.

It's totally dark, too. No lights anywhere, inside or out. Seems more than just dark, though. With all the other houses on the street lit up and lived in, Phoebe's house seems aggressively dark. No car in the driveway.

Mommy must still be partying on the lake.

"Are you okay to be here alone?" Carol asks, turning in her seat to face Phoebe.

Phoebe releases a quiet sigh. "Yeah. I'm used to it by now. Pretty much here by myself all the time, anyway."

Carol nods. Her face darkens.

"Thanks, though." Phoebe opens the door. She leans back in. "Thanks for everything tonight. Both of you."

"It was our pleasure," Carol says.

My eyes are still glued to the sheer darkness of the situation in front of the car. Carol nudges me.

"Oh, um, yeah." I clear my throat as if that'll make things less awkward. "You're welcome. Thanks for your help with the project. Those drawings are going to put ours over the top."

Phoebe nods, a ghost of a smile on her exhausted face. She makes to close the car door but stops halfway. She scans the darkened front of her house and peeks her head back inside.

"Um, Ms. Odum? I was, uh, wondering if—well." She swallows hard. "If you guys do carve those pumpkins, can I, um. Can I come and help?"

She gasps at her own forwardness and slams the door before Carol can answer. She jogs, following a little brick pathway that disappears behind the house. A few seconds later, a light pops on inside. Through the front windows, I can see her close the back door and lock it behind her. She crosses the kitchen and plops down at the table.

Carol backs out of the driveway, and before the car rolls out of sight, I look over and see Phoebe with her face resting in her arms on the table.

The bright pink headband bobs up and down with her sobs.

CHAPTER 12

Carol and I are both are still a little sleepy as we pull into the parking lot. We got home a little after 10:00 last night, which isn't, like, earth-shakingly late, but I don't think either one of us had an easy time getting to sleep after that. I tossed and turned for hours, all the time hearing the creaking of her bed as she did the same.

It's weird. Back in the days of Ugly Me, I used to lose sleep over evil Headband Girl because of the mean looks and nasty things she said to me. But now that I'm turning over this new leaf and she's been transformed into Phoebe being dumped off and left alone by her party animal mom, I'm losing sleep over her in a whole new way. Still hard for me to believe I'm feeling anything other than hate for her.

Can't help but wonder if I'd have been able to feel for her before coming to live with Carol. Even if I would have known about her real story, would I have been able to give half a crap, or would I have still been so wrapped up in my own pain that I'd have had no room to care about anyone else's?

Are we all like this, or am I just a terrible, selfish excuse for a human being?

The parking lot is almost full when we pull in. We're on time, but for Carol, "on time" is uncharacteristically late. She's the kind of lady who feels already late if she's not, like, 20 minutes early for everything.

Carol shifts into park and turns off the ignition. "Well?"

I give a little start. "Well, what?" This is weird. Kind of feels like I'm in trouble for something I don't realize I've done.

She sighs. "You've been awfully quiet since last night. Barely said a word after we dropped Phoebe off." She reaches over and puts her hand on mine. "You don't have anything to say?"

I study the ridges and valleys on the back of her hand. The lines are deep and all crisscrossy, telling the story of a life of hard work out in the dirt. I shrug.

How can I put into words what I'm only just learning to feel?

"Okay, dear." She lets go of my hand and opens the door. "Whenever you're ready." Her voice carries a disappointed weight.

I can't let her walk into work like this. Her job is hard enough without me making her feel bad by being all Mutey McSadface.

"Thank you," I blurt out.

She stops and pokes her head back into the car. She cocks her head and gives me a curious look.

"For setting up this whole thing with Phoebe." I sigh. "You were right. I needed it. It's just, I don't know. A lot to process, is all."

"Oh?" Carol chuckles. "Is this the elusive 'teenager admitting that the adult was right about something' I've heard about but never seen in the wild?"

I smile. "Maybe, but don't get used to it."

"Noted." She clears her throat. "How about after school we go get those pumpkins we talked about last night?"

—*ele*—

Phoebe looks as exhausted as I feel. Me coming in right in the nick of time doesn't leave us any time for chitchat. Probably a good thing, too. I'm not ready to debrief on that heck of a last night, and I'm pretty sure she isn't, either. Best to play it slow. I get out my binder and flip to yesterday's notes, happy to have something to distract myself with.

If I can stay awake, anyway.

I used to function in a perpetual state of exhaustion. Most nights were a terror- and hunger-fueled crap fest of uncomfortable little snoozes that eventually melted into hazy daylight. Up and at 'em. Time for a glorious new day. A chance to do all this fun stuff over and over again. A good night was a couple hours of uninterrupted sleep mixed in with half a dozen little shallow snoozes. I'd come to school wanting and needing nothing more than a warm, safe place to curl up in.

But the school authorities thought differently. To them, all I needed was more math, more science, parts of speech, state capitals, and all kinds of other stuff jammed into my exhausted brain. Principals and counselors would interrogate me on what time I went to bed, what my nighttime habits looked like, what I *chose* to do instead of sleep like a good, responsible little girl.

But I knew if I told them what was really going on, that I spent most of my nights shaking like a leaf in a thunderstorm while God knows what was happening in my house with God knows who, that the hungry animal in my gut was so angry it wouldn't let me sleep, then—well—I just knew I couldn't tell them.

So I told convenient little lies and gave fake little apologies and made fake little promises to change my bad little behavior. They tried to help correct my wayward ways by punishing me, giving me detention and in-school suspension when I'd sleep in class.

Fat lot of good that did. How was punishing me supposed to change all the things happening around me that I couldn't control? Punish me a million times, give me detention every day, lock me in a jail cell with other delinquents, beat me with a stick, string me up by my dirty undies from the flagpole. None of that could change what was happening to me once I left those doors every day.

Well, now I think of it, maybe "function" is being way too generous.

Let's just say I somehow "survived" in a perpetual state of exhaustion.

I look back at Phoebe. I catch her in the middle of a ginormous yawn. She blinks long and slow, then notices me, gives a little wakey-wakey head shake. Darkness encircles her eyes, and her signature headband—purple, this time—is all wrinkly and askew. She's not wearing layers of makeup today, but it doesn't really hurt her looks. Enhances it, really. Makes her look more human, like less of a clown. I didn't bother much with the mirror this morning, so I'm sure I look even worse than she could ever possibly look.

For the first time ever, she doesn't roll her eyes at me or give me that wrinkled-nose, "Did someone just fart?" kind of look. Her eyes are softer, kinder. Even through the exhaustion.

I hope mine look the same to her.

I give a little nod with an upturned mouth corner for good measure. She returns it. Not the emotional embrace of BFF's, but it'll do. Much better than before.

"I'm sorry your mom cares more about partying with boys than she cares about hanging with you. I pretty much know exactly how you feel."

That's what I hope my little look communicates, anyway.

I turn back and try to focus on Mr. Worsham's class. Now that I have the relative brainspace to focus on something other than survival, school isn't that bad. Some of the stuff is actually kind of interesting...sometimes. I mean, they still try to cram way too much pointless stuff into our heads. And trust me, there's not that much room up there what with all the messed-up teenagery junk banging around all over the place. It's like all the teachers forgot what a confused, hormonal mess we all are when we're 13 years old and think our noggins are just some kind of empty, eager containers waiting to be filled with useless dates and names and equations and boring books and Latin names and God-knows-what else.

Plus, even my youngest teachers like Ms. Morris didn't have to deal with all the new crap us kids have to these days. It mostly comes from everyone being so addicted to stupid phones and the Internet. When they're trying to get us to pay attention and remember a bunch of stuff, I don't think they consider that our brains are already overstimulated by the little devices almost everyone is carrying around in their pockets these days. Even kids like me who don't have phones aren't excluded from the insanity, what with everyone showing stupid viral videos around and talking nonstop about all the online drama.

The big trend now is for kids to take videos of themselves breaking things and stealing stuff in the bathrooms. It's driving the principals and custodians crazy. Wouldn't be surprised if they shut down the restrooms entirely and make us hold it all day. I'd be on board with that if it meant these jerks would stop stealing all the soap and toilet paper. That's what the teachers are competing with these days. I hate to say it, but even the most entertaining teacher is at a major disadvantage.

I never thought I'd say this, but I'm glad that idiot stole my phone and that Carol refuses to even think about the possibility of letting me have one. It might be against some kind of foster care rule or something, but even if it wasn't, I don't think she would go for it.

Which is a good thing. Even without a phone, all the stupid stuff I hear about is exhausting. I mean, if the *trend du jour* isn't outright mean and awful and evil, then it's at the very best just plain idiotic.

And without a phone, I'm immune to all the awful things people say about me when I'm not around.

But anyway, I've got a little more space up in the gray matter these days, so school isn't as much of a chore as it used to be. Enjoyable at times, even.

Unfortunately, my body's already been sort of rewired by having a healthy routine, and last night's sleeplessness is hitting me hard.

I wrestle my attention back to the front of the room. Mr. Worsham is going on about plant cells. He must really be into the subject because he's in enthusiastic teacher man mode. What that really means is that his voice is just a little less monotone than usual, and the last word of each sentence rises in tone. It's like everything he's saying is a question or something.

His dream-glazed eyes are focused on some spot in the distance above our heads. "What I find so amazing about plant cells is that they are capable of creating their own sustenance." Seeing him staring off into the distance gives me an almost undeniable impulse to follow his gaze, even though I know he's just spacing out. "Imagine how much different our lives would be if our cells could create their own nutrition."

I'm in the process of nodding off, but that idea grabs my attention.

If only.

How different would my life have been over the last however-many years if I'd just been able to go bask in the sun and fill my screaming, empty belly? Breathe deep, soak in the warming rays and just feel full and bloated and happy without having to rely on anyone else. How many meals would I *not* have missed? How many days would I *not* have stumbled through in a hangry haze of boiling-over emotion? How many homework assignments would I *not* have missed because I'd been too preoccupied with just surviving another night?

My tired mind finds a wandering path and follows it away from Mr. Worsham's lecture. I try to make my way back, but the golden October sun beckons to me through the windows.

CHAPTER 13

A few stubborn leaves still cling to the late-October branches of the oak in our front yard. They chitter-chatter in the cool breeze, dancing against the backdrop of a picture-perfect blue sky. I lie under the tree, hidden in the pile of leaves I made with my little pink toy rake. At some point, it had this Barbie sticker on it, but rain and sunlight tore it away. All that's left of it now is a jagged little mountain-shaped smear of leftover white sticker stuff.

Dad used to be the one who piled up the leaves with his big green man-sized rake. He'd whip up these ginormous piles and we'd jump and tumble and laugh until we couldn't anymore.

I haven't laughed like that since they took him away. As if that policeman took all my giggles and he-haws and shoved them in the back of that cruiser with Dad. They're all locked up tight now, just like he is.

Only my eyes peek out of the pile. Took me, like, almost an hour to scrape up enough leaves for a pile big enough to hide the whole me. I'm bigger than I used to be, but I somehow feel smaller, like I'm shrinking each day with little parts of the old me flaking off and scattering in the breeze.

A sheen of sweat is making the leaves stick to my back. Worked up quite a lather getting these things together.

But it was worth it.

My new bed is soft and warm. It surrounds me with the bittersweet scent of autumn, hiding me from all the everything. I just wish it could hide me from the hurt, from the Ugly that wants so bad to creep up from deep inside. It's stalking me, this scary new version of me. Hunting me down, waiting until I'm finally weak enough and angry enough and hurt enough to let it take over.

But at least for a few minutes, I've got my own little world. The Ugly knows I'm here, but I feel it creep back into the shadows a bit.

I just lie still and breathe slow and deep. Cool autumn air fills my lungs, and I hold it there, feeling it swirl and spin inside me like magic fairy dust, filling me with a sunshiny something. When I finally breathe out, the bad feels whoosh out of me on my hot breath.

I haven't felt this okay in a long time, and a smile threatens to cross my chapped lips.

I rinse and repeat, breathing in the good and huffing out the bad, just lying here in this silence until the shadows get longer. I don't care that some sort of creepy crawly is making its way up my calf. All I care about is staying still in this little leaf haven I've made for myself, by myself.

Maybe I can do this. This whole life thing, I mean.

Or maybe if I'm really lucky, the thing crawling on my leg will bite me and kill me with its venom.

I shake free of that thought and refocus on the blissful nothingness of these leafy breaths. Eventually, the critter crawls its way into the leaves. Probably better off that way. If it bit me, I'd be more likely to infect it with my venom.

Breathe in, *two, three, four.*

Hold, *two, three, four.*

Breathe out, *two, three, four.*

Hold, *two, three four.*

In the distance, a cricket starts up its nightly chorus. The sun dips lower, blue fading to gray. In the neighborhood, parents call to playing children.

Time to come inside for dinner.

But I stay here.

Breathe in, *two, three, four.*

There's no parent, no dinner waiting for me. Just hunger and pain.

Hold, *two, three, four.*

I don't even know where Mom is right now.

Breathe out, *two, three, four.*

But even if I did, it would still be the same. Maybe even worse.

Breathe in, *two, three—*

"—anda Lewis!"

I bolt awake with a sleep-heavy, drooly snort. It sounds jet engine loud in the mostly silent room. A smattering of giggles taint the air behind me.

I blink the sleep away to meet the disappointed gaze of Mr. Worsham. He's looking down at me through bushy eyebrows, hands on hips. I slurp a drooly stream off the corner of my mouth.

He releases an impatient huff. "Am I boring you, Miss Lewis?"

I try to shake the sleepy out of my brain. I try to tell him that the stuff he's talking about is actually super interesting to me, but my words are all gummed up by sleep and leftover dream. What comes out sounds more like the guy who used to walk my street talking all kinds of gibberish to himself.

"I—uh—nono*ish*not*that*—Miiiiiiiister Worshmmm."

The chorus of tee-hee-hees behind me grows, threatening to break out wild and take over the world. Mr. Worsham silences them with a harsh look and keeps teaching. Thank God. Back when Ugly Me used to have free reign to fight and curse and threaten, I'd have gone straight into crazy mode. She'd have turned this whole little thing into a real steamy dookie-show and gotten me kicked out of school for a few days. That, or at least locked up down in in-school suspension. Which I would have refused to go to, which would have then gotten me kicked out.

You know, fight or flight.

Or for me, fight *then* flight. Then maybe fight again.

Now that I think of it, most of the trouble I found myself in came from Ugly Me going all apey over little things that were said or done to me. By snotty kids. By teachers. By people who were supposed to be looking out for me.

Not that I'm trying to play all innocent. I'm so totally not. Not by a long shot. I've come to fully own my past, present, and future craziness.

But all I'm saying is I never really went out of my way to unleash Ugly on the innocents.

Anyway, I'm super glad Mr. Worsham imposed *Silence of the Teacher*. I'm trying so hard to keep Ugly Me away, and I don't want to go anywhere near back to where I was. I'm trying, like, super hard to do better. Trying like I've never tried at anything in my life. I know there are non-crazy ways to handle it when other people are jerks, but I don't know what those are just yet.

Maybe I'll get there one day.

But do I dare to hope?

All hoping has gotten me before are black eyes, empty bellies, and broken hearts.

It's at precisely the wrong moment my stupid brain decides to tune back in to Mr. Worsham.

"—then please raise your hand."

Without thinking or even having the itsiest clue what the heck is going on, obedient little me shoots her scrawny, scarred hand into the air.

"Oh, great!" Mr. Worsham's voice carries a distinct hint of shock. "And your partner is...Miss Matson, correct?"

I give a slow nod.

What in the ever-loving, holy heck did I just volunteer for?

"Fantastic!" His smile widens. "I'll let the principal know right away."

I look back at Phoebe.

She looks like she's about to vomit.

CHAPTER 14

"Wait...what?!" My worn-out little heart is slamming against my ribcage, threatening to break out like that baby alien in the movies. I imagine a trail of tiny, bloody footprints glistening on the still-shiny hallway floor. "Like, in front of teachers and kids and parents and everything?"

"Yes!" Phoebe's face is somehow pale and flushed all at the same time. "Weren't you listening?"

My eyes fall and find an empty tampon wrapper. I nudge it with my toe and bite my lip. It skitters across the damp floor like a dried-up leaf.

"Umm, not exactly." I bend over, pick the thing up, and wad it into a ball. "Kinda spaced out for a bit."

She rolls her eyes and leans against the countertop. She gives a little growl and presses her palms against her eyes.

"So I suffer because you decide to space out and volunteer us for some God-awful public humiliation ritual?" She releases her hands, leaving behind red splotches on her face.

She's a mess, but she still manages to be gorgeous. And to top it all off, I find out that she's not completely, totally evil.

Where is the justice in that?

At my absolute best, I'm a scrawny, frizzy-haired monstrosity with a too-big nose and more than my fair share of zits.

The sudden flush of a toilet makes us both jump. It's jet engine-loud among this tense semi-silence. An eighth-grader with a purple-tinged undercut walks out of a stall, gives us a "what the heck is *your* deal?" cocked eyebrow, and leaves without washing her hands.

Yuck.

Yes. You heard it here first, boys. Girls are gross, stinky mammals, too.

I make a careful study of the balled-up paper in my hand. It's decorated with little pink, green, and blue cartoon leaves that look like they're swirling in the breeze. Why the heck do they waste ink on crap like that? What's the point? Why do all these companies think all women want are frilly, girly things? I mean, does it matter what's on the wrapper of the thing I'm about to shove—well, you know what happens with those.

If they absolutely have to print something on there, why not inspirational quotes? Jokes, maybe? Fortunes like in those nasty cookies?

You are destined to have a miserable, bloated day.

Embrace the suck.

Don't worry. Menopause in only forty years away.

"Sorry," I mumble. My voice is near-cry shaky. "I'm really, really sorry."

That's all I can manage to squeak out because I'm afraid if I say much more I'll burst into tears.

Crossing my arms, I lean back and feel something wet seep through and soak a cold line right across my bony butt. I hiss and jerk away from the sink like I've been stung by a bee. The sudden movement sends my feet slipping in a puddle of yuck. A cold, wet floor rushes up to meet me. My noggin bangs itself on the edge of the counter on my way down. I land hard on my derriere.

I oof out a big breath and some kind of pained animal noise rushes out with it.

Old habits rush back hard. My head and booty hurt like crazy, but I bite back the pain and brace for the laughter. I raise my arm like a shield to hide my face from the cell phone videographers wanting a few quick likes on Tiksnapstagrambook or whatever the app du jour is. In my experience, the laughter and the online shares hurt more than the broken bones.

Fight mode engaged.

But the laughter doesn't come.

"Oh, my God!" Phoebe's hands grab my shoulders. She's shaking. "Are you okay?"

The sudden shock of unexpected kindness breaks my tears loose. I go from zero to 60 in a second, boo-hooing like an overgrown baby. A feelings tornado breaks loose inside me and blows out of my eyes, nose, mouth. Phoebe pulls away for a second, floored by the sudden outburst. I feel her uncertainty hang in the air like a thick fog. I don't blame her. I mean, the scars I dug into her face still haven't healed. And now here we are.

It's been a hecka crazy few days.

But then she does a thing that takes me by complete surprise.

She hugs me.

Plops down on the slimy floor right next to me in her fancy jeans and wraps me up. For, like, a half a second, I think about pulling away. I still have a hard time trusting people that are nice to me for no reason. Cautious skepticism or downright hostility is more my comfort zone.

But being with Carol these days has made me realize that it's okay to let people be nice to you. That not everyone is out to rob me blind or try to feel me up or be nice to me to just suck up to my mom.

I lean in, and then the really big boo-hoos start. Over and over I whispercry, "I'm sorry, I'm sorry."

She just shushes me like a little mommy. "It's okay. It's okay. It's not that big a deal."

That brings on more tears, and I squeeze her back. Pretty soon, she's crying, and we dissolve into a big, hormonal pile of uglycrying crazygirls.

On a disgusting school bathroom floor.

Even if we could talk, I don't think we'd say anything. What words are there when you've got all the feels rushing out in a snotty tsunami at the same time? Years of built-up hurts, fresh new hopes, old worries, new worries, all the what-ifs and hope-nots and if-onlys—everything all together all at once.

And the darndest thing?

It's the same for her. She doesn't say it, of course, but I can feel it. Feel it in the way her shoulders shake, the way her head bobs up and down on my neck, in the wetness of her tears mingling with mine as they run down our cheeks.

This girl who I used to think had this perfect little picturebook life with the perfect hair and the perfect clothes and the, you know, *not* starving all the time thing. She's right here, too, just crying out all these same feelings.

These tears, these fears, these hurts, these hopes—they unite us, blend us together in the beautiful, messed-up right here, right now on this wet bathroom floor.

The thought makes me hold her harder, squeezing like I'm trying to wring all the saltwater out of both of us.

Are we all like this?

Are we all different versions of the same person, just human chameleons covering pain and joy and fear and hope with different brands of the same skin?

We cry together long after the tardy bell warns us we're going to be in deep doo-doo if we don't report to class on the double. I don't even remember where I'm supposed to be right now. It won't be long until the authorities seek us out and drag us away from this moment.

But I don't care, and Phoebe doesn't seem to care, either.

In the distance, the intercom calls our names, its staticky, authoritarian voice demanding our presence in class.

We don't have long. The staff always check the bathrooms first. For good reason. The adults really aren't as stupid as we like to think they are.

We pull away. A shiny strand of crysnot stretches between us. It glistens under the harsh fluorescent lights. As we pull further apart, it thins and stretches until it breaks. It whips apart and leaves shiny streaks on both our shirts.

We share this grossed-out look with our red, puffy eyes, but pretty soon I crack. It starts out as a shy giggle, but before long we're both cackling.

The laughter is so loud we don't hear the footsteps in the hallway until it's too late.

CHAPTER 15

B usted.

The crime: skipping class.

The guilty parties: two seventh graders.

The sentence: afternoon detention.

Appeal: denied.

Appeal of the denied appeal: denied, with prejudice.

Appeal of the denied appeal of the denied appeal: denied, with extreme prejudice

———*ℓℓ*———

The detention room smells like a dirty sock took a dump on a gallon of spoiled milk. Maybe they're trying for a creative new form of discipline. Submission by gross-out.

If so, I can't blame them for trying, since, you know, the old ways were soooo effective.

Cue heavy eye-roll.

I wonder if any of the higher-ups ever bother to think about the fact that it's the same kids over and over again who get suspended, locked up in in-school suspension, or thrown in detention.

I mean, I don't know how many times I spent all day sleeping in this room or wandering the streets while I was suspended.

Did it fix me?

What was that thing some famous person said about insanity? Something about doing the same things again and again but expecting different results?

Apart from the smell, the detention room feels like home away from home for me. I mean, I practically lived here last year. It's this damp, windowless room on the bottom floor of the school. The walls are lined with these black cubicles covered in graffiti. Inside each cube is a broken-down desk facing the wall. The desks are like a rusted, splintered time capsule. It's like whoever furnished this room dug through some forgotten closet and pulled out a desk from each era since the beginning of school time. Reject furniture in a reject room for reject kids.

Very welcoming.

I waltz in and plop my butt in one of the wooden and metal desks from the '60's. The varnish on the seat has been worn down by countless booties over the years, leaving behind a perfect butt-shaped light spot of bare wood. The metal frame is all spotted with rusty spots, and the top desk part sits at a weird angle and squeals all old and angry when you put any weight on it. Seems like a strange first choice, but I've been in this place enough to know to avoid the ones with the cracked plastic seats. They look harmless enough, but the cracks have a way of giving you these wicked pinches on the back of your thighs when you least expect it. You also have to avoid any seat with loose rivets on the place where your back goes. Sit in one of those for even half a second and your hair gets tangled up so tight that you walk away with a painful bald spot when you stand up. With all the hair and skin I've lost to these desks, my DNA is probably all over the place in here.

I may be old hat at this, but Phoebe is in a whole new world. Except for exotic magic carpet rides with a handsome wannabe prince, she's getting an intimate tour of the smelly spot between the school's unwashed toes.

Welcome to Rejectland.

She takes a timid step into the room and wrinkles her nose. Today's unlucky warden, some burly new teacher guy with a carpet of frizzy black hair sticking out of the back of his polo shirt (yuck!), swivels in the squeaky old teacher chair and grunts at her to park it. I don't know this one. Must be new here. Dollars to doughnuts he's a coach of some sort—the hotheaded kind that yells at the kids and throws his clipboard. A real role model for today's impressionable youth. You know the type.

In the interest of new-leafing it, it's maybe not super fair of me to make assumptions given what I've been through. But some stereotypes really hold up.

Phoebe is shaking. Her doe eyes scan the room and land on the only other occupant—some little kid all turtled up in his dirty hoodie fast asleep in one of the pinchy desks. The hoodie is decorated with anime guys from one of the shows where the characters hit each other with fireballs and swords and laserfists and boulders but still manage to survive at the end of each episode. Burlyman follows her gaze.

"Hey!" he yells in a boomy fake-deep manvoice. Extra testosterone added. His hairy neck goes a deep, ragey crimson. "I told you to keep your head up, kid!"

Kid.

Ugh. It's like this guy took a training course on how to make kids feel unwanted. Must have made an *A*+. Top of his class.

Pencils and pens go rolling as he slams his fist on the desk. Phoebe and I jump. She gives a little *eek* and scoots double-time to the nearest seat—one of the hair-pullers. Big mistake, but I can't say I blame her for it. Panic choice. Been there more times than I can count.

Hoodie Kid doesn't move. He's stuck fast in la-la land. Dead to the world.

Been *there* more times than I can count, too.

Not that I ever really *wanted* to sleep in class and get screamed at for it, but most times I couldn't help it. I mean, I always knew that math and English and history and all that are important—*Education is the Key to Unlock the Future!*. School motto and everything right there on a faded banner outside the office. But try to tell an adolescent brain that just spent a sleepless night being scared out of its skull that instead of sleep, what it really needs is to learn how to write a haiku or memorize the capitals. See where that gets you.

Biology wins out every time.

Used to be you could stick me somewhere even halfway safe and I'd be out like a light. My body, brain, booty craved sleep and safety so bad it hurt, and no threat or consequence could shake me. Beat me, lock me up, make me stay all night long—nothing mattered but getting those Z's.

I know all that sounds harsh, but I get where the teachers are coming from, too. They've got the school board and the media breathing down their necks all the time about test scores, test scores, test scores. The dumbing-down of America. What's the world coming to when today's kids can't even name all the presidents or recite the atomic mass of the elements? But what those bigwigs seem to miss is that most of us kids aren't the blank slates they think we are. Not even close. I'm starting to realize that so many of us are so broken you'd cut your fingers to ribbons trying to write anything on our jagged surfaces.

The teachers are as tired and stressed as us kids are. Maybe worse. Too bad we can't just all get together, admit that this whole thing just kind of sucks for everyone, and get to work on gluing each other back together.

Neckhair stands up with a huff. The ratty chair squeals against the floor, sending shivers up my spine. Phoebe shudders. He stomps over to Hoodie Kid, picks up the front of his desk until it looks like the poor kid is going to fall out of the thing backward, and lets it go. The desk jams back onto the floor with a crash. The impact jars Hoodie Kid's head, and the hollow thunk of his forehead hitting the wooden desktop fills the room.

I explode.

CHAPTER 16

Phoebe retches loudly as she reaches her hand into the cold, sticky pumpkin guts. I dissolve into a steaming pile of giggles. She pulls her hand out, and a slimy stream of seed-spotted orange goo follows. She squeals and shakes her hand like she's trying to get rid of a man-eating spider or something. Totally, hilariously frantic. The stuff flies everywhere, plastering her face and hair. A big, fat seed sticks to her cheek like one of those prison teardrop tattoos. She gags again, a big, open-mouthed one.

My giggles morph into an all-out belly-laughing fit. Rolling on the ground laughing. Carol wisely made us do this pumpkin carving thing outside. We're ten minutes in, and the grass around us is already littered with goop, seeds, and chunks of pumpkin. It's like a murder scene in one of those crime shows where the detective dude always makes some sort of punny wisecrack about the poor victim at the beginning of the episode.

"Looks like this pumpkin really got jacked up.*"* Roll opening credits.

She also wouldn't let us have actual knives, so instead we have these tiny orange-handled saw-like things she bought at the grocery store when we picked up our pumpkins. They're a bit flimsy, but they get the job done. And we don't have to worry too much about, like, chopping off our little digits. I mean, bloodstains on the jack-o'-lanterns would be a nice, spooky touch, but still.

Another smart move. This lady knows what she's doing.

I finally manage to control myself long enough to finish sawing around the stem of my pumpkin. Mine's this greenish-white, lumpy, deformed thing with these little warty growths all over it. Carol wanted me to get something a little more well-formed and orange and traditional, but this chunky reject caught my eye. It was the last one in the giant cardboard bin. Looked so lonely and castaway I couldn't resist.

My spirit pumpkin.

We hear a *bang-ding* from inside as Carol slams the phone onto the receiver. It's one of those old-but-not-that-old types. Still has a cord and an actual bell inside, but it's new enough to have buttons instead of that weird wheel thing that some really ancient relics have. The cord is, like, a thousand feet long and can reach almost all through the house.

I guess the conversation is over.

My shoulder still smarts from where Mr. Neck Hair literally dragged me up to Carol's classroom after I gave him a piece of my mind.

Well, more like a whole chunk of my mind. And I shoved it down his throat, really. With prejudice.

I don't remember exactly what I said, but Phoebe says it was a pretty good speech. What part she could understand through all the screaming, that is. A lot of stuff about walking a mile in some shoes with a healthy side of "You don't even know_____."

I only cursed twice.

Not bad for a near-Ugly Me outburst.

Carol walks outside and slams the screen door behind her. Phoebe and I freeze and share a wide-eyed uh-oh look.

"Young lady," she says in her teacher voice as she points an arthritic finger at me. She waggles it and hits me with a red-hot laserstare.

Oh, man. I'm screwed. My self-preservation mode starts to kick in. My body tenses, ready to spring away like a scared animal. I mean, I know I shouldn't be yelling at teachers, but that jerk—

"I am so proud of you." Her face softens and melts into a warm, gooey smile. I let out a big breath. Didn't even realize I'd been holding it.

Good one. She really got me.

She pads around the mess and pulls me in for a hug. My head presses into her hip. I catch the faint scent of freshly baked cookies—a warm, comforting scent.

"Just got off the phone with Mr. Sullivan." She runs her knotty fingers through my hair. "I think it's safe to say he won't be pulling a stunt like that again."

A smile crosses my lips. My shoulder might hurt for a few more hours, but I've been the recipient of a few good old-fashioned Carol Odum tongue lashings. He's going to be sore for days.

Her hand continues toying with my hair. Phoebe notices, and she gets this weird look on her face. Not, like, a *bad* look or anything. But she's definitely thinking about something.

"Not that I give you permission to unleash your unbridled opinions at will, and you will certainly apologize for your use of crude language," Carol chuckles. "But some situations certainly warrant speaking up. A large part of maturing is learning when to speak up and when to keep your head down."

I dive into the hug and put my arms around her. I probably smear her dress with pumpkin ick, but I don't care. It feels so good for someone to take my side—well, mostly. All except for the choice bits. Out of the corner of my eye, I see Phoebe frown and look down at her pumpkin. She's got this faraway look in her eyes, and I can tell it bothers her to see Carol hugging on me.

Maybe it's just weird for her to see the mean old math teacher this way, but I can't help thinking it's something else.

Carol releases me and pulls an old metal lawn chair over. Her squatting cross-legged in the grass days are long over, but she doesn't want to be left out of the fun. She grabs up the third pumpkin—a spotless, orange, magazine-perfect specimen—and makes short work of cutting off the top and scooping out the guts. Her old, knobby hands move fast and easy, putting our young, awkward ones to shame.

We spend the next hour giggling like three little girls as we cut and carve under the fading October light. Sips of warm spicy apple cider chase the chill away. Phoebe never does get used to the gooey stuff, so she adds a few more gags here and there. And every time she does, our giggles turn to belly laughs—even hers. When we're done carving and Carol lights the candles, we've got a trio of goofy, gap-toothed smiles shining back at us in the twilight.

A chill breeze stirs the leaves overhead, and some of them tumble down, finally releasing their tentative grips. They float down, soft like giant, colorful snowflakes.

The sick and dead falling away, making room for healthy new springtime leaves to paint the world with green again.

The three of us stand there in silence, feeling the autumn feel, warmed by the cider and by our own closeness. Carol puts an arm around each of us.

I smile.

Phoebe bursts into loud, sobbing tears.

CHAPTER 17

Steam from the hot cocoa wisps toward the kitchen ceiling. I twirl the spoon and watch the half-melted marshmallows spin and whirl, dancing and bobbing like happy little bathers. I stare, silent and hypnotized. It's been a whirlwind of a day, and every part of me is completely exhausted. But these thoughts are swirling in my head like those marshmallows—around and around and around and never stopping.

I should've been in bed an hour ago, but sleep won't come.

Phoebe never really said much after her breakdown. We chatted a little about some random stuff through dinner, mostly a bunch of "get to know you"-type stuff that Carol kept asking to keep the silence hidden in the shadows. But for the most part, she was like a deflated balloon for the rest of the night—just all flat and lifeless and nothing coming out. Her house was dark and empty when we dropped her off. She sat the jack-o'-lantern on the bare front stoop before she went in. In the rearview mirror, the thing's smile taunted me. It seemed so forced, fake.

I used to wear that smile a lot.

I wonder how many of Phoebe's smiles have been jack-o'-lantern smiles? She'd always seemed so cocky and self-assured. How much of that was a costume just like my angry, "I don't give a crap about nothin' or nobody" routine.

"What do you think *that* was about?" I asked as soon as Carol pulled out of her driveway.

"You mean to tell me you *don't* know why Phoebe became upset?" She looked over and shot me a cocked eyebrow. "I would have thought a girl with your background would pick up on those things."

I let out a deep sigh. "Sorry to disappoint. I only recently started to, like, actually care about other people, remember? I'm still practicing this whole empathy thing."

That made Carol chuckle. She nodded. "Well, I think that, very much like you, Miss Phoebe is coping with trauma. And it's quite clear that our activities tonight stirred some strong emotions. Now, whether these feelings are tied to good or bad memories is something you might be able to talk to her about sometime."

I nodded.

"But for now," she continued, "be thankful that Phoebe felt safe enough with you to let her emotions be free. It takes a great amount of trust to do that, you know."

I nod again. No words. Wow. So super talkative. Shut up, Blubbermouth.

Carol pats me on the shoulder and pads down the hall. She must be exhausted, too, what with doing all the teacher stuff and the older lady stuff and the taking care of me and all my messes that she does. Never complains a bit. Just gives and gives and does and does.

I suddenly feel a rush of guilt hit me like a cold wave. Not that I'd really know what waves feel like, what with never having been to the ocean in my life. Never been very far from this place.

All I do is take and take. I mean, I do some chores and pretty much clean up after myself, but that's just stuff people, like, just *do*. Nothing special. Maybe it's time I gave something back to her. Did something really nice for her.

But what?

I push the whole Phoebe emotional breakdown thing to the back of my mind and add this conundrum to the mix. It needs to be something big. Like, really big. After all, the lady pretty much saved my life, for crying out loud.

But what?

I have no money of my own, so buying something is out of the question. Besides, even if I had money, Carol isn't really a stuff kind of person. If I bought her something, she'd most likely make me return it so I could save the money. I sit and think hard until the cocoa stops steaming. If I were a cartoon character, you'd be able to see the gears turning like crazy and the smoke pouring out my ears.

The sound of running water cuts through my thought process. Carol's in the shower.

And suddenly a thought pops into my head. *Ding!* Light bulb. I leave the mug of cocoa cooling on the kitchen table. I tiptoe down the hallway, going into full-on ninja mode. Have to act fast if I'm going to make this work.

I have to stand on my tiptoes to reach the little wooden chest on the top shelf of Carol's closet. This feels so dirty, this invasion of her privacy, but it's for a good cause. Surely whatever's in this little box will give me some sort of clue as to what I can do for Carol. I grab the thing and slide it toward me. When it's a little over halfway off the shelf, the thing tips over, catching me off-guard with a surprisingly heavy weight. My stick-thin arms fail me, and the thing drags me to the floor in a heap. I almost cry out as the thing lands on my fingers, the sharp wooden edges smooshing them into the carpet. I pause, breathless, praying that the sound of rushing water hid the sounds from her.

The sounds of showering continue from down the hallway.

I let out my breath in a hot, stinky *whoosh*. Yuck. I really need to brush my chompers.

The box is held closed with this little tarnished gold-looking latch. I slide the catch, and the box pops open, spilling papers onto the floor. With shaking hands, I riffle through them.

Tears spill down my cheeks.

CHAPTER 18

There's something about coming back to school in the evening that just feels so incredibly...*wrong*.

The parking lot was half-full when we pulled in, and parents, staff, and kids were pouring in through a door propped open with one of those plastic blue chairs with the metal legs that's so very unmistakably schoolish. I mean, have you ever seen one of those in the wild?

Me, neither.

It's like everything in a school has to come from some special, probably overpriced school catalog or something. I imagine principals and teachers sitting on the can and thumbing through the latest issue of *Public Schools "R" Us* and eagerly circling items for their wish lists.

Parents and kids clot the main hallway, mingling and chatting and just kind of milling around. The Fall Showcase doesn't start for another thirty minutes, so no one's in a huge hurry to start sweating in the non-air-conditioned auditorium. It's a minefield of bodies, and Carol and I have to weave and bob like boxers to make our way through. All the lights are off in the empty classrooms, and without glaring fluorescent lights and stressed-out teachers and complaining students, they seem so empty and sad. Plus, it's getting dark outside. This place looks so different only lit up with artificial light—haunted, almost. Shadows in places they shouldn't be.

I've been here, like, a million times, but coming back in this way makes me feel like an alien exploring a strange new land.

We make our way to a classroom next to the auditorium's backstage door. It's where all of tonight's unlucky victims gather. Carol deposits me and pads down the hallway, ducking backstage. Probably going for a front-row seat to my public humiliation ritual.

Thrown to the wolves.

There are a couple of weirdos who actually look excited to be here, but when I look around, I mostly see poor saps like me who would rather have their toenails yanked out than get up on stage in front of a swampy auditorium full of teachers and parents and whoever else comes to these things. One such oddly enthusiastic freakazoid is dressed up like an elementary school George Washington and is pacing around rehearsing lines in a very bad British accent. Off-key warm-up music from a trio of sixth-grade band geeks with clarinets lends an extra doomy vibe to the whole scene. There's an eighth-grade guy dressed in an untucked dress shirt plopped in one of those blue school chairs, tap-tap-tapping his knee with a rolled-up paper. His other knee bounces up and down so fast and hard it feels like the whole floor is shaking with it. He gives off such a nervous vibe that I can feel my heart rate rise just looking at him. I give him a second look, letting my eyes linger for just a second—he'd be cute except he's got this wisp of one of those gross, fuzzy teenage boy mustaches. Looks like dirt smeared under his nose. Some girl in the corner is holding a papier mâché model of a moon phase chart. The color of her face matches the full moon in the center of it. Looks like she could blow chunks at any second. Maybe if she's lucky, she will.

I know the feeling.

I wonder if Carol would let me out of this thing if I made myself up-chuck the brown beans and cornbread we had for dinner. Side note: brown beans and cornbread are totally an old person meal, but they are freaking amazing, especially on a chilly evening like this, and especially, especially if the beans cook all day and all night with all kinds of fat meaty bits added in for flavor.

Anyway, there's no way I would try that because Carol would see right through it and would probably make me wash my face, rinse my mouth, and get up on stage with a vomity shirt. Guess I have to wriggle into my big-girl pants and just do this thing.

My eyes keep flitting to the doorway. Phoebe isn't here yet, and she's got the poster we made. As much as I kind of don't care about this thing, I was hoping to have a few minutes to look things over and rehearse our spiel one last time. I'm totally prepared to make a fool out of myself, but as long as I'm doing this, I want to minimize the embarrassment as much as possible. Bonus points if it actually resembles something like a success.

I sit down and try not to channel Faux Mustache Guy's nervous energy while I wait. The noise around me blurs into a dull roar as the time ticks by. The air in the room gets steamy and funky with all the nervous sweating.

Still no Phoebe. Doubt threatens to creep in, but I tamp it down. She'll be here.

At some point, someone comes on the intercom and tells all the people in the hallway to find their seats in the auditorium. The distant rumble of chattering bodies shifts, and I can soon hear them through the back wall. I glance back at the doorway. Still completely Phoebe-less. Devoid of Phoebes.

My heart starts to pound. A familiar feeling creeps in.

Ugly Me.

Fight or flight.

A breathless dark-haired woman with one of those Madonna headsets like in the old music videos scoots into the doorway. She's got a clipboard clutched to her chest. The light glistens off the beads of sweat on her forehead. I sweep my hand across my own brow, and it comes away wet.

"Alright," she says between deep gulps of air, "are you all ready?"

A wave of doubtful murmurs courses through the room—with a couple of annoyingly enthusiastic "Yeahs" sprinkled in.

I say nothing. My words are stuck behind my hammering heart. I peer around the woman, hoping to see Phoebe's trademark headband.

Nope.

Ugly Me's voice pipes up, all whispersoft but loud at the same time.

Where is she? Was I wrong about her? Has all this new warm-and-fuzzy friendy stuff just been some elaborate prank? Was she planning this the whole time? Would she have volunteered us for this if I hadn't blundered into it for her?

I think about all the jeers and snippy comments. The ugly names. The "I smell something awful" looks she and her posse shot my way.

Did I really expect all that to go away just because we found out how screwed up we both were? How could I have been so stupid?

"—Lewis and Phoebe Matson with...umm, a science presentation about leaves?"

I snap back to reality and lock eyes with Microphone Lady. I give a slight nod.

"Okay," she says, glancing down at her clipboard. "Is your partner here?"

I shake my head.

"Hmm." She scribbles something on the clipboard. "I'll just bump you down to give her some more time. You can go last. That okay?"

Thank God for small miracles. That'll give me some time to plan my escape.

I nod.

"Great!" She lasers me with a toothy smile.

I try my best to return it, but the corners of my mouth barely creep upward.

A round of applause rumbles through the wall, and Microphone Lady gives a little squeal as her earpiece crackles to life.

"Oh! Looks like we're ready." She motions to Off-Brand George Washington. "Let's go!"

She shuffles out of the room with our nation's first leader in tow. His enthusiasm has suddenly faded, and his face is a pale green. If he hadn't been annoying everyone in the room for the last 30 minutes, I'd be tempted to feel sorry for him.

The minutes ooze by as the room slowly empties. Still no sign of Headband Girl. With each passing second, Ugly Me grows louder, more insistent.

I'm finally left alone as a couple of ballerinas follow Microphone Lady out of the room.

You're in for the humiliation of a lifetime! I'll bet Headband Girl and her friends are in the audience right now, their phones out and ready to record. By the time you're offstage, you'll be all over their socials!

I try to beat her back, clinging to a shred of hope.

A round of applause from the other side of the wall means it's my turn next. My heart rat-a-tat-tats as my brain floods with panic juice.

Little scared deer me is ready to spring.

I poke my head out of the door. The coast is clear, but not for long. I only have a few seconds. I take a breath, steeling myself for a sprint to God-only-knows-where-but-anywhere-is-better-than-here-ville.

But when I take that slow breath, something else comes with it.

Memories of last night. The things in Carol's box. I could hardly see through the tears to put it back in time to avoid being caught.

Pictures of a younger, happier Carol. A baby girl in a pink, frilly dress. A smiling toddler with spaghetti all over her face. A hundred more pictures like those, memories of absolute joy.

But at the bottom of the box, a tearstained funeral program. A four-year-old baby girl plays with the angels now.

Rest in peace, Eleanor Miranda Odum.

Ugly Me retreats as the tears fill my eyes again.

If Carol can go through that and keep living, I can make it through whatever comes next.

CHAPTER 19

M y English teacher's chipper voice echoes around the auditorium from the broken-down speakers dotted around the auditorium.

The '80s called. It wants its ginormous beast of a sound system complete with cassette tape thingy back.

"Up next is Miranda Lewis and Phoebe Matson with," she looks down at the paper in her hand, "a presentation about the exciting miracle of leaves."

She tries to make it sound as un-lame as possible, but even Ms. Sunshine can't put a very shiny spin on that one. I'm all at once embarrassed for her, pre-embarrassed for myself, and feeling sorry for the audience for having to sit through this after all the other shenanigans have come and gone.

I don't hear any groans or boos, so that's good at least. They may be bored crapless, but they'll maybe do it politely.

She gestures offstage toward me, and Microphone Lady nudges me. My legs suddenly go numb, and my heart, already beating a billion beats per second, speeds up double-time.

And maybe a little bit of pee comes out.

But I can neither confirm nor deny that.

Somehow my feet carry me into the spotlight. Polite applause echoes around the room as I shield my eyes from the sudden ocular onslaught. I blink away stars as my stunned eyes scan the crowd, but the glaring white of the spotlight only allows me to see a crowd of dim, faceless shapes.

That's probably not a bad thing. It'll be easier to ignore all the little *tee-hees* and obvious hatewhispers hidden behind hands. Out of sight, out of mind.

Or so they say.

Whoever made that saying up clearly didn't go to middle school. I can't tell you how many sleepless nights I spent worrying about things that were out of sight but certainly not out of mind.

The microphone is too tall, so I have to tilt it down. The little holder thing is tight, so I have to really jam on it. I pull too hard, and the thing slams down, dumping the microphone onto the floor with a booming *thump* that echoes around the whole auditorium. The speakers squeal, and even my blinded eyes can see people everywhere grimacing and covering their ears.

Wow. Off to a great start, Randi. Totally killing it.

I bend over and pick up the microphone with a shaky hand. A few muffled giggles dance across the crowd. I don't even try to mess with the stand thing again. I just hold the microphone to my mouth and start talking.

"Hello, my name is—" another deafening squeal interrupts me. I just now realize I'm practically holding the microphone inside my mouth. I can taste the foamy cover.

More giggles—less muffled this time—and a couple of full-blown laughs.

I pull the microphone away from my mouth a little and try again.

"Um," my voice comes out all dry and scratchy in a timid monotone. "My n—name is Miranda L—Lewis, and we—I mean—I am going to tell you all about the interesting world of leaves."

I'm going just like we rehearsed, but I don't remember it sounding this *lame.*

"Leaves are...um...leaves are...um...leaves..."

My breath is coming in ragged gasps. My hand is shaking so bad I'm afraid I might knock my teeth out with the microphone. The auditorium is dead silent now—much worse than the laughter. This means they can see I'm about to lose it.

My half-blind eyes begin to dart around the room, frantically searching for an escape route. In my head, sirens scream and red lights flash.

Wee-woo! Wee-woo! Warning! Warning!

Possible escape route spotted. A glowing exit sign just offstage to my right. My body tenses, ready to spring...

But then I glimpse Carol in the front row. She sees me looking and gives a big smile and a gentle nod.

Come on, girl. You've got this!

She says so much without saying any words at all.

I plaster on a smile, clear my throat, and let out my finest imitation of a silly teen girl giggle.

"Whew! What a disaster!" I give an exaggerated eye roll. "Right, people? I mean, have any of you ever seen a worse start than this?"

A smattering of polite laughter ripples around the crowd. I read in a magazine somewhere that making fun of yourself can sometimes make you feel like less of a complete dope and can trick people around you into not hating you. That doesn't work in the cutthroat world of teenagerdom, but it seems to be working now. I can sense a collective release of pent-up breath as people realize they're not about to see an uncomfortable episode of the

Scrawny Girl Implosion Show. I'm surprised to find that their sudden ease knocks some of the tension out of me, too.

I can do this.

In the front row, Carol gives another encouraging nod.

I grip the microphone tighter, noticing my hand isn't shaking quite as hard.

"So, anyway," I say, punctuating with a chuckle, "my partner and I were supposed to get up here and regale you with a presentation about leaves, complete with a cute little speech and visual aids." I'm surprised at how easy the words are coming now. "But it looks like you're stuck with just me and whatever words I decide I'm going to spit out." A big smile. "So buckle in, people."

Some genuine laughs at that.

Okay, okay. I can, like, *really* do this.

"You know, this thing about the leaves was the first school project I actually, like, cared about in a really long time. Maybe ever. At first, I thought it was because I like plants and stuff," I lock eyes with Carol. "But right at this moment, I'm realizing why I *really* cared so much about some stupid science presentation."

I scan the crowd again. No sign of Phoebe. I glimpse a couple of her crew sitting in the crowd with their parents, but I don't catch any sneers or ugly looks.

"But I guess before I really get going about leaves, you need to know some things about me." I take a deep breath. "You may recognize me as *that kid*. You know the one. The one you tell your kids to steer clear of. The one you see walking the streets alone and wonder where the heck the parents are. The one that makes you shake your head and ask what this world is coming to."

The auditorium is dead quiet.

"The one with the dirty clothes who leaves behind her stink wherever she goes. The angry one with the short fuse who screams and curses. The one who wants to fight about everything. The one no one trusts as far as they can throw her. The kid the other kids laugh at and talk about when they think she's not listening—and sometimes when they *know* she is."

What is quieter than dead quiet?

I'm not sure, but that's what the crowd is now.

The words keep welling up from deep down. I can't stop them. Now that they're flowing, these words, unsaid for so long, rush out in an unstoppable flood.

"But what you may not know is that I'm also the kid who watched her dad get dragged out of the house by the police and get locked up. The kid whose mom is an addict and cares more about where she's going to get her next fix than about her. And who, consequently, is now also locked up." My heart is pounding, and my hand is trembling again. "The kid who doesn't know where her next meal is coming from but knows it's definitely not coming from home." Tears form at the corners of my eyes. "The kid who wants nothing more than to be loved and accepted but has been through so much that she's afraid to let anyone in. The kid who acts tough like she doesn't care but really she just wants to feel safe and fed and warm like a newborn baby."

A few sniffles break the silence.

I clear my throat and sniff. I dab my eyes with my sleeve. "So yeah. That's me." I look at Carol. She's wiping her eyes with a crumpled tissue. "Or *was* me, anyway. Before someone saw past all that and give me a chance. A chance to turn over a new leaf." I smile down at Carol. "And I think that's why this project meant so much to me. Because when you really think about it, leaves are a miracle. You know, when I was really little, before—before the bad things started to happen—my dad would rake up these enormous piles of leaves in the front yard, and I would jump and laugh and play and he would rake them up again and again no matter how many times I'd scatter them, and..."

My voice trails off as I remember. Something about saying all this aloud is doing something. I feel a loosening inside me, a long-stuck something letting go.

"...and then the cold and snow would come, and the leaves would get slimy and rot and the tree would be all cold and naked and dead like a skeleton..." I blink and refocus my eyes. I'd almost forgotten I was baring my soul to a packed middle school auditorium. "But then spring would come, and—and do you know what?" A smile spreads across my face. My eyes find Carol. Fresh tears form. "New leaves." Tears drip down my cheeks. "Fresh new leaves right where the old ones used to be. Green. Healthy. Ready for a new life. A new start."

Flashes of white in the audience. Carol isn't the only one employing tissues.

"We're like that, too, you know. I mean, I didn't really think about it until just now, but we have seasons, too. You know? Some seasons last longer than others, but it's all temporary." I chuckle and wipe my eyes again. "Me? I had a really, really long winter. Years long. Thought it might last forever, even. I'd almost given up." A smile spreads across my face. "But all I really needed was a little sunshine to wake up my new leaves."

I lock eyes with Carol. Some of the people sitting around her notice, but I don't care. I want to call her out, scream her name, tell the world what she's done for me. She deserves that recognition.

But I don't. She wouldn't say so, but I know deep down she'd hate it. Hate the attention, the recognition.

I can give her that.

"So I guess what I'm saying is, you never know what other people are going through." I think about Carol, carrying around hidden pains for years upon years. Of Phoebe, hiding a broken life behind a mask of perfection. "So don't be the frost that kills their leaves. Be the sunshine that grows the new ones."

That's it. I'm done. Speech over.

I go to put the microphone back, but the stand has magically moved ten feet away. Either that, or my feet moved me without my knowing. Instead of fooling with it, I just bend over and set the microphone down gently.

As I walk offstage, the auditorium explodes.

Applause and cheers follow me out into the hallway.

CHAPTER 20

When we pull onto Phoebe's street, I can immediately hear the *thump, thump, thump* of too-loud party music. Vehicles are jam-packed into her driveway like toy cars in a shoebox. The block is lined with cars, too. I notice most of them have Eden College decals and parking tags.

A thirty-something woman throwing a rager for college kids.

Pathetic.

Most of the overhead lights in the house are off. The whole place is lit up with colorful, flashing lights.

Carol sighs. Its heavy sound fills the car with disappointment. I'd insisted on Carol driving out here to check on Phoebe. I wasn't mad that she didn't show. Just worried.

"I had higher hopes for Ms. Phoebe." She shakes her head slowly. "But it seems like she made her choice. I'm sorry, Miranda."

I nod. I want to agree, but I'm not so certain.

I mean, I know the evidence sure is damning. Certainly seems like Phoebe stood me up for this party. I mean, I've never been to one of those T.V. college parties, and a bunch of drunken, sweaty bodies bouncing around some poor sap's living room sounds like a nightmare to me. Although I suppose it might be more appealing to some people than getting up in front of a packed middle school auditorium. But there's something inside me that feels all squirmy.

I've got a feeling there's more to this story.

Carol clicks her tongue in that scolding *tut-tut* way and swings into a neighbor's driveway to turn around. The porch light flicks on, and a grumpy-looking face scowls out of the little window beside the front door. I'm sure they're none too happy about the kegger down the street. As we pass back by Phoebe's house, the feeling in my belly grows. I start to feel antsy, squirmy.

Did she really choose this? Is Phoebe really more like Headband Girl than I thought?

No. I refuse to believe it.

"We have to stop," I say suddenly, grabbing Carol's forearm.

The tires give a little yelp as she slams on the brakes with a startled foot. "What in the world are you—"

I don't hear the last part of the sentence because I'm jetting out of the car and pounding the pavement toward Phoebe's house. My heart races as the booming music swells in my ears. I feel like I'm going to have a full-blown panic attack, but I keep pressing on.

I don't recognize the thing driving me on. It's not like Ugly Me or any version of myself I've ever seen before.

When I open the door, the swampy odor of sweaty bodies and alcohol almost knocks me over. The music is deafening, and the living room is a sea of costumed people all grinding and mashing together like garbage from a drifting shipwreck. I've never seen so many girls dressed in trashy versions of normal things in my whole life. Trashy firefighter with a helmet and a coat that barely covers her butt. Trashy policewoman with shorts so short

I can practically see all the business. Trashy student witch with a long robe and basically nothing else. Oh, and about a zillion trashy nurses, the OG trashy costume.

The guys are mostly dressed in discount store costumes. Cheap pirates, cheap vampires, cheap serial killers from all sorts of horror movies.

Of course, no one is here to win a costume contest.

I don't have time to stop and feel sad for these girls putting their bodies on display like racks of food at the store for all the hungry shoppers.

I'm sure I'll feel it later, though.

Strobe lights punctuate the darkness, making everything stutter and jolt. Combined with the smell, the noise, and the heat, it makes me nauseous. I stop and bend over, fighting the urge to retch right there on the beer-stained carpet. I feel a heavy arm come to rest across my shoulders.

"Hey cutie. Had enough?" His slurry voice is right in my ear. I can smell the stink of his drunken breath. "Want me to take you out for some air?" He pauses. I can practically hear his evil grin widening. "I'll take real good care of you. Promise! You won't be—"

My bony elbow connects with his gut and cuts off his sentence. He doubles over as I dash away. Discount surgeon with bloodstained scrubs. He empties his stomach loudly, and the crowd around him protests at the new, unwelcome mess.

My nausea is gone, chased away by adrenaline.

I've got to find her.

I weave through the crowd, calling her name. I'm bumped and jostled like a sock in the dryer, and I can barely hear my own voice over the noise. I make my way through the main level, shouting for her and trying to ask about her, but drunken ears can't understand me.

I can't find her anywhere. With each passing second, I grow more and more desperate. I call for her over and over like a mother calls for a lost child.

Tears of panic threaten to break free. I hold them back.

Be strong! The last thing you want to do is lose it in a place like this!

I reach a set of stairs that stretches up into darkness. As I climb, muffled sounds reach my ears over the fading music behind me.

"Phoebe!" I shout, my desperate voice traveling up into the darkness. "Phoebe!"

I sprint into the darkness. Pain explodes in my legs as I trip and bark my shins on the edge of a step. A warm stream trickles down my left leg and into my sock.

I hear a squeal from somewhere in the blackness. Something cuts it off short.

No time. I can hurt later.

My legs pump, fire blazes anew with each step. I swallow the pain and keep going.

I finally reach the top. A strip of dim light under a door at the end of the hallway.

A muffled cry for help.

Phoebe's voice.

I dash down the hall, screaming her name at the top of my lungs.

"I'm coming! I'm coming!"

Beneath me, the party rages on, its costumed revelers oblivious to the real horror show upstairs.

I reach the door. Grab the knob with shaky hands and turn it.

The door is locked! The door is locked!

My brain threatens to shut off as my heart hammers my ribs to bony shards.

With an animal scream, I pour all my rage and my fear and my everything else into one desperate kick. The flimsy door gives way and crashes open so fast and hard the knob jams into the drywall and sticks fast.

Phoebe's on the bed, struggling beneath a drunken Dracula. He's attacking her like a hungry pit bull. His hands and mouth are all over her as she screams and squirms.

I don't even think. I just act.

With a howl like an enraged animal, I jump on his back. He's so much bigger than I am, but I don't care. I tear into him with nails and teeth. He's the vampire, but I'm the one who bites. He howls and tries to throw me off, but I hold on, biting and clawing at his face and neck with a fury I've never felt in my life.

I've been mad before, but this is *different*.

This is not an Ugly Me hating the world and lashing out with sharpened talons.

He rolls off the bed and lands on his back on top of me. He's the one screaming now. He yells and squirms, and I'm crushed beneath his weight. But I don't relent. I'm going to rip his stupid face off if it's the last thing I do.

His screams turn to thick, drunken sobs. But I don't feel sorry for him.

Suddenly, the overhead light flicks on, flooding the room with blinding brilliance.

Carol's panicked voice cuts through the noise, calling my name.

I let go of him, and he rolls off me, sobbing and holding his face. He curls up on the floor. I stand on shaky legs as my eyes adjust to the sudden light.

Phoebe's sobs mingle with her attacker's. She's still fully clothed, thank God, and Carol rushes over and scoops her up in a big hug. She shushes and coos as she rocks her back and forth like an infant. Phoebe wraps her arms around Carol's bony frame and dives into her, squeezing and gasping, breathless with hysterical sobs.

My whole body starts to tremble as a sudden ice bath washes over me and extinguishes my blind rage. I pile on to Phoebe and Carol, adding my hugs, my warmth, my tears.

Phoebe's attacker stands with a groan. He has blood pouring from a thousand gashes on his face, and he sports a wicked bite mark on his neck. He limps out of the room, trailing sobs behind him.

He will wear those scars for a long, long time. Probably forever.

But what scars will Phoebe carry? And for how long?

No. I push those thoughts away. Those are for another time.

Because now, now is for tears of relief, for hugs, for gratitude.

Because now I have my friend back.

My friend.

CHAPTER 21

The next few hours are a blur. Lots of flashing blue lights. Lots of police. Lots of questions. Some answers.

The guy who attacked Phoebe got arrested. A bunch of the other college kids got hauled off, too. Turns out a lot of them were underage. Also turns out that Phoebe really wanted to come to the showcase, but her mom refused to drive her to the school. She'd been sulking in her room avoiding the party when the drunk guy wandered in and...did what he did.

Phoebe's mom is in a ton of trouble. She probably didn't know half the kids were too young, but that doesn't matter. She should have known better.

After a long, weepy conversation between Phoebe's mom, Carol, and the police, it's decided that Phoebe will come stay with us for a few days while her mom sorts things out and tries to get a grip on her life.

I really, really hope she can turn over a new leaf, too.

By the time we make it back to Carol's house and get cleaned up, it's, like, two in the morning. We're all dead tired but too wired to sleep, so we curl up on the sofa. The kitchen radio's on.

There's not much talking. That will come later. We're all just glad to be together and okay in this moment.

Phoebe yawns and leans over, snuggling her head into my lap. I stroke the soft waves of her hair. My fingers trace the outline of her headband, and a smile crosses my lips.

Headband Girl.

Life sure has a way of throwing curveballs.

In the kitchen, a gravel-voiced country singer croons about being a millionaire because he has love in his life.

I smile and lean my head back, staring out the tall window behind me. A tear spills down my cheek.

For the first time in my life, I feel so very, very rich.

In the sky above me, a brilliant blanket of stars twinkle through the branches of the tree in Carol's front yard.

The branches are bare now, but I smile knowing that new leaves are coming.

Want more?

Check out the free prequel story!

Click below to receive a free eBook and audiobook version!

https://www.jestamper.com/sign-up

Made in United States
Orlando, FL
15 June 2024

47920826R10067